BABE
CONQUERS
the WORLD

Babe Didrikson practices sprinting for the U.S. Track and Field Championships in 1932.

BABE

The Legendary Life of

CONQUERS

Babe Didrikson Zaharias

the WORLD

Rich Wallace and Sandra Neil Wallace

CALKINS CREEK
AN IMPRINT OF HIGHLIGHTS
Honesdale, Pennsylvania

Calkins Creek
An Imprint of Highlights
815 Church Street
Honesdale, Pennsylvania 18431
Printed in the United States of America

ISBN: 978-1-59078-981-0
Library of Congress Control Number: 2013953471
First edition

10 9 8 7 6 5 4 3 2 1

Designed by Barbara Grzeslo
Production by Margaret Mosomillo
Titles set in Bell Gothic and Aachen
Text set in Frutiger

*To the pioneering women athletes
of the twentieth century,
who persevered beyond measure*

*Winner Babe holds the
Tam O'Shanter golf trophy.*

ACKNOWLEDGMENTS

When we threw our hat into the ring and served notice that we were writing a book about Babe Didrikson Zaharias, we recruited an international team of all-star supporters. We gratefully thank the following contenders for knuckling down with us as we uncovered invaluable information about our star player.

Penny Clark and Charlotte Holliman at Lamar University's Mary and John Gray Library, who organized what we needed from the Babe Didrikson Zaharias Collection so that we could pull no punches during our stay in Beaumont, Texas.

W. L. Pate Jr. of the Babe Didrikson Zaharias Museum and Stephanie Molina of the Beaumont Convention and Visitors Bureau.

Stephen Anthony, secretary of the Gullane Golf Club in Scotland, who rolled with the punches until we finally struck gold in locating spectators who'd watched and met Babe when she won the British Women's Amateur in 1947. Thanks to Susan Penman, captain of the Gullane Ladies' Golf Club, and Gratian Andrew and Rena Craigs for sharing their colorful stories and fond memories of Babe.

Fred Dahlinger Jr., world-champion circus historian and curator of circus history at the John and Mable Ringling Museum of Art. Fred brought a fresh angle to Babe's childhood by helping us solve the identity of her neighbor who performed the iron-jaw act in the circus.

Darwin Morris, Dustin Hightower, and Stephanie Soule, who gave us ringside seats at the Tyrrell Historical Library Archives in Beaumont.

Juanita Galuska, who worked tirelessly in our corner at Calkins Creek; fearless copy editor Joan Prevete Hyman; and extraordinary art director Barbara Grzeslo.

And finally, Calkins Creek editor Carolyn P. Yoder, for refereeing and championing the book to the final round.

CONTENTS

Babe, shown in 1932, broke records and stereotypes wherever she went.

OPENING PITCH

Babe Didrikson donned a baseball uniform and rode to the pitcher's mound on the back of a donkey. She threw a fastball to a man with a heavy beard. The crowd roared with laughter.

Babe was the only woman in the game. After pitching a few innings, she jumped into her car and drove to the next small town as part of the team's two-hundred-game "barn-storming tour."

It was a humiliating turn for the world's greatest woman athlete. Two years earlier, in 1932, she'd been an Olympic hero. Now, as a professional athlete, she spent lonely days driving across the country and sweaty evenings in gimmicky games with a donkey-riding ball team. The games were more for laughs than competition.

But it beat typing letters for a living. Babe was earning her way in sports, and no other woman had succeeded at that. The baseball tour helped her stay in the spotlight while she searched for a "real" sport to conquer.

Babe Didrikson Zaharias wasn't a feminist and she wasn't considered feminine. Babe wanted to be the world's greatest athlete. Her unstoppable drive changed sports for women.

Babe's natural ability helped her dominate every sport she tried. Her intense desire to win kept her training as long as necessary to punch holes through records or change the way the games were played.

Sportswriters ridiculed her, saying she was more like a man. Organizations tried to block her and other women from competitive sports. School gym teachers warned girls not to be like Babe.

Babe didn't complain and she didn't back down. The world needed to catch up to her.

We've known about Babe for most of our lives. We never had a chance to meet her, but her story helped lead us into careers as sports journalists.

One of the first books Rich read in school was a biography of Babe. The next day, he was hurdling over boxes and other obstacles in his backyard, trying to be like Babe. He has enthusiastically participated in sports his entire life and written many novels that inspire kids to do the same.

Sandra wasn't a professional athlete, but she spent years interviewing them on TV for ESPN. Babe's achievements, coupled with her unflappable drive and bravery amid any adversity she faced, also enabled women journalists like Sandra to become sportscasters. Babe forced the world to take notice and realize that women deserve to make a living in sports.

It still isn't easy. On Sandra's first day as a National Hockey League reporter, she was confronted by a male sportswriter who strongly believed that women had no place in sports. "Welcome to the end of your career," he snarled. Shaken by his remark, Sandra prepared her feature, determined to prove him wrong.

Coincidentally, he was from the *New York Daily News*, the same newspaper that had produced Paul Gallico, Babe's most vicious critic. Gallico had written that Babe was an "it," as if a successful woman athlete couldn't really be a woman at all.

Sportswriter Bill "Tiny" Scurlock—Babe's longtime friend—once wrote, "Just where fact ends and fiction begins regarding Babe is anybody's guess."

We've done our best to stick to the facts, but Babe was a storyteller. Not everything she said or wrote in her extraordinary life turned out to be true. One thing is certain: she dominated every sport she tried, and she did it with flair, guts, humor, and a "never take no for an answer" determination.

This is the inspiring story of how she fought through these obstacles and conquered them to become the greatest woman athlete of all time.

—*RW* and *SNW*

"Babe never saw a person in her life, male or female, she was afraid of."

—Godfrey Choate, childhood friend

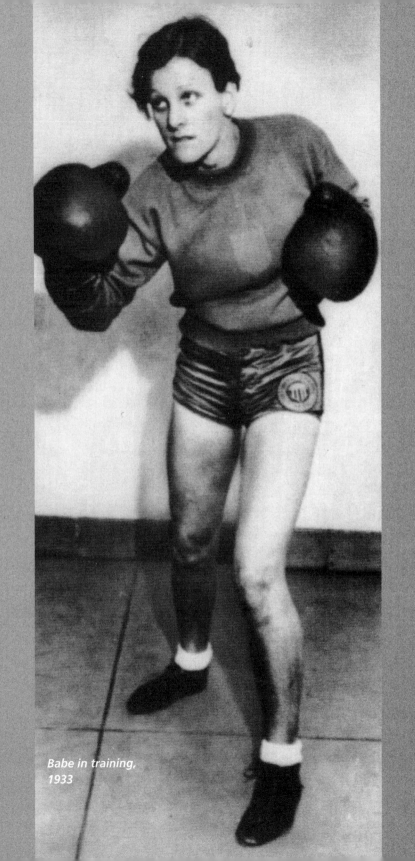

*Babe in training,
1933*

BABE
VS.
THE BOYS

"All my life I've always had the urge to do things better than anybody else."
—Babe Didrikson

"If she beat me, I could never make myself congratulate her. I'd just say, 'I'll practice some more, Babe, and I'll getcha next time.'"

—Raymond Alford,
Babe's neighborhood competitor

The Lucas gusher, 1901

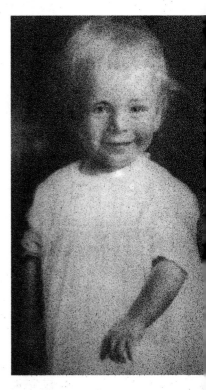

Mildred Ella "Babe" Didriksen as a toddler in Port Arthur, Texas

Just before dawn on June 26, 1911, an explosion rocked Port Arthur, Texas. The blast on a barge threatened to send the coastal city up in smoke. Wharves caught fire, and residents rushed to save the city from ruin.

It was called "the most disastrous conflagration in the history of Port Arthur." But the fire may not have been the most significant event of the day. Babe Didriksen was born within minutes of the blast.

The explosion was on a barge named *Humble*. Babe would grow up to be anything but humble. She would become the greatest woman athlete of all time.

Babe was born a few blocks away from the burning wharves in a house that her father had built. Ole Nickolene Didriksen was proud to have finished it in time for the birth of his sixth child. Ole (pronounced *Oo-leh*) was curious about his newest daughter's name. His wife, Hannah Marie, had decided to call the newborn Mildred Ella. It sounded more American than Norwegian.

Six years earlier, Ole had sailed from Norway to the Gulf of Mexico on a tanker. The Texas oil boom was in full swing after drillers struck oil nearby on a salt mound called Spindletop Hill. Port Arthur rushed to keep pace. Dredging operators—some of them convicts wearing balls and chains around their ankles—battled alligators in the mosquito-filled waters. They were deepening the port for oil tankers like the Norwegian ship Ole was on.

Babe's father wasn't an oilman. He was a shipbuilder and cabinetmaker from Norway, with a thirst for seafaring adventure as strong as his woodworking skills. Ole also needed to go to sea to earn extra money.

In Port Arthur, nobody seemed to mind being covered in the residue from the greenish-black oil that hung in the air. Including Ole. He liked the hot climate more than the harsh winters in Kristiania, Norway (known today as Oslo). Other Norwegians were immigrating to America because of crop failures and their country's sinking economy. Most settled in farming regions of the Midwest. As a craftsman, Ole believed he could earn a better living in a town benefitting from the new oil industry. Soon, he sent for his wife and three children.

Hannah's reaction to Port Arthur was different from that of her husband's. Smelling "nothin' but oil, oil, oil," Hannah cried when she saw the oil tankers and refineries belching out grimy smoke.

Hannah struggled with her new country and its English language. She focused on her family instead, including American-born twins, Louis and Lillie. Two years later came Mildred Ella.

Babe (left) stands arm in arm with brother Bubba and sister Lillie.

"How is it with this girl?" Ole asked Hannah about their rambunctious daughter. "I'm afraid no crib I can build is going to hold her." Hannah fondly called her "Min Babe" (my Babe).

The wealth Ole had hoped for never materialized. In 1915, by the time Babe was four years old, Ole, who the children called Poppa, went out to sea again.

A HURRICANE HITS

Hannah, or Momma, was nine months pregnant. A slow-moving August hurricane took aim at the Gulf Coast as she was about to give birth to the seventh and final Didriksen child. Babe and the other children hurried to bring chickens and ducks inside. By nightfall, all power and communication was lost.

After her son had been delivered with the help of a town doctor, Hannah and her children were left alone. Huddled in an upstairs bedroom, they were grateful, at least, that Ole had built a two-story house. Water rushed from the canal into the streets. It gushed into the Didriksen home, rising nearly to the ceiling on the first floor.

"We was so scared," said Lillie. She was six years old when the storm hit. "Everything was gone in the flood. Ducks, chickens, trees, beds, money, dishes, everything. We didn't save nothin.'"

Left in the marooned city without fresh water while Momma's icebox floated in the kitchen, the Didriksens somehow

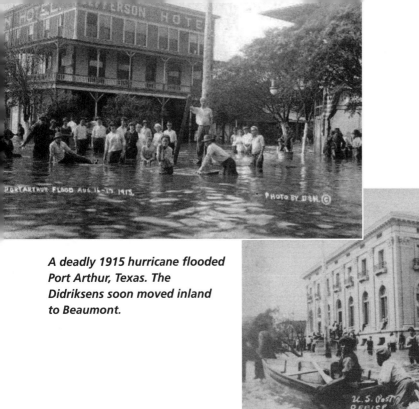

A deadly 1915 hurricane flooded Port Arthur, Texas. The Didriksens soon moved inland to Beaumont.

survived. Momma named her new son Arthur Storm, but the children called him "Bubba."

After the hurricane passed, Babe was eager to swim in the flooded streets. She was upset that she wasn't allowed to leap from the second floor into the water. "Some of us opened the upstairs windows and jumped in," Babe's brother Louis remembered. But little Babe could only watch.

The house that Ole built survived, but he didn't want to risk another hurricane. When he returned from the sea, Ole moved his family twenty-two miles inland to another Texas port city, Beaumont, which was connected to the Gulf by the Neches River.

NOTHING BUT OIL, OIL, OIL

Life wasn't any easier on Beaumont's Doucette Avenue—the neighborhood where the oil refinery workers lived. Momma took in washing to help pay the grocery bills and was in charge of the family's finances. As Babe explained, "Poppa let Momma handle the money in our house."

On one end of dusty Doucette, trains rumbled as tanker cars, loaded with oil, pushed north. On the other end stood the Magnolia Refinery, Beaumont's largest. It let out a steady, hissing stream of smoke and fumes, four and a half blocks from the Didriksen home.

In between, Babe and Lillie—Babe's sister and most loyal friend—usually played until past dark, and Momma kept "callin' and *callin'* to get us home." Babe stayed out the longest and often got spanked with a broom, before Momma "hugged Babe up." Unlike Momma, Babe loved living in the steamy, smoke-belching south end of Beaumont. She was happiest outdoors, roaming the trolley-tracked neighborhood barefoot.

At night, Babe listened to Poppa's seafaring adventures. Babe never tired of Ole's exaggerated tales of being shipwrecked and stranded on desert islands with wild monkeys, or saving others from the swirling waters of death. "What a bang we used to get out of his stories," Babe said. Listening to her father helped turn Babe into a storyteller, too. Throughout her life, she enhanced the stories of her own accomplishments to make them more entertaining.

The Didriksen family loved to gather on the front porch after dinner. Pictured in front are Lillie, Babe, and Louis. In back are Ole Jr. and Ole Sr., who is holding Arthur, called Bubba. Two older sisters, Dora and Esther Nancy, are not shown.

But Ole's stories didn't bring in money. His income was uncertain, and the family struggled. Work was sporadic. Ole helped build ships made of yellow pine for a short while during World War I, but the war ended in 1918. He set up a furniture-refinishing business in the backyard, but it didn't produce much income.

Boiler Avenue
April 23 1903

By 1903, hundreds of oil derricks stood an arm's length apart on Boiler Avenue near the Spindletop gusher. Explosions and fires were frequent, but the money earned from oil production made it easy to rebuild.

THE CHAMPION GUSHER

The Lucas oil well blew on January 10, 1901, south of downtown Beaumont, Texas. Situated on a hilly acreage christened Spindletop Hill because of the shape of a nearby cypress tree, the well sent one hundred thousand barrels of oil into the air for each of the nine days it gushed. The landscape became a slick, black lake before the well was capped.

Within months, 138 oil derricks stood about an arm's length apart on fifteen acres surrounding the gusher, harvesting the greatest oil discovery the world had ever known. Black-gold fever swarmed over Texas, much like the California gold rush a half century before.

Workers walked along the wood plank sidewalks with sponges tied over their noses and mouths so they wouldn't pass out from the fumes. Several years later, Babe and her gang didn't bother with handkerchiefs. They played in the streets all day and swam in the river behind the Magnolia Refinery, located at the end of Babe's street.

The smoke-belching Magnolia Refinery wasn't far from Babe's house. Babe often swam in the Neches River behind the oil refinery.

THE NEIGHBORHOOD PEST

As Babe grew older, she grew fearless. To avoid the heat of the east Texas summers, she'd swim in the nearby Neches River, bucking its riptide currents. Babe risked being bitten by water moccasins and alligators. Not Lillie. Though Lillie was two years older than Babe, she was timid. According to Lillie, Babe was developing a personality "full of devilment."

That meant climbing onto the roofs of the trolley cars that rolled down Doucette. Babe would unhook the pole that kept the trolley on the track and watch the car slide to a stop. One night, she did that to a trolley that her father was riding.

Trolley cars ran throughout Beaumont, including on Babe's street.

Poppa saw the culprit. But because it was Halloween, Babe was disguised in her brother Louis's clothes. She ran home and hid under the porch. Poppa blamed Louis. But Babe finally confessed.

Babe became known as "a little Tartar and the neighborhood pest," said Emma Andress, who lived nearby. But if Babe got caught, she was "always honest and would admit any wrongdoing." One dangerous prank she played on her brothers and sisters was to stick a match between their toes when they were sleeping. Then Babe lit the match. Luckily, she never burned down the house.

At age seven, Babe entered Magnolia Elementary School a few blocks down the street. She soon became the school marbles champion and began looking for new challenges. Around this time, Babe decided to spell her last name another way, changing *sen* to *son*. The new spelling served notice: Babe Didrikson was different.

Even at a young age, Babe refused to accept what a girl was supposed to be like. She didn't play with dolls or try to look pretty. Babe preferred having her hair short to avoid getting it in her eyes while playing baseball or marbles. So she hacked off her chestnut-colored hair, wearing it bobbed and chin length in a style known as the Dutch Boy. Although she was small, Babe took part in rough games and sports. It wasn't enough for Babe to participate. She needed to win. Arguments with her brothers sometimes ended in fistfights.

It was rare for young girls to play sports in 1918, but Babe caught a lucky break at Magnolia Elementary. The school's principal, a woman named Effie Piland, saw that Babe was "too good to compete with the girls" and "too far ahead of them." So instead of playing "sissy" games like drop the handkerchief or clap-in-clap-out with the girls, Babe was allowed to play sports with the boys. Babe needed to sweat and jump and run. But more than anything else, she was always trying to be the best, and she wanted to be challenged.

It was different with the boys at the neighborhood sandlot. They didn't want Babe in their games because she was a girl. If Babe was going to be the best at all sports, she would have to prove to them that she belonged.

Babe performed in the Magnolia Elementary School band. She's fourth from the left in the top row.

BEATING THE BOYS

The sandlot was next to the trolley barn on Doucette. In this lot, it didn't matter if you were poor. What mattered was how well you played. To the boys, the lot was the closest thing to the big-league stadiums like Boston's Fenway Park or Detroit's Navin Field. This was the place to dream about being a professional athlete, like Babe Ruth and Ty Cobb and the other baseball heroes the boys followed in the newspaper.

For Babe, there were no professional women athletes to look up to. But she desperately wanted to be a part of the baseball games. Babe had decided that she wanted to be an athlete.

Raymond Alford, one of the top players on the sandlot, kept the "diamond" mowed before the games on Saturdays. Babe waited for Raymond and the others to decide if she could play. Finally, they put Babe "in right field, like you always did the worst and weakest ones." Babe caught the ball. She played well all day. Soon Babe was among the first chosen. She played shortstop, third base, and pitcher. Babe proved that she was a versatile player and often the best. "Babe was different," Alford said. "Once you saw her play, you didn't mind having her around."

Like the boys in the sandlot who became her peers, Babe would sometimes display her temper with her fists. "Babe never saw a person in her life, male or female, she was afraid of," said Godfrey Choate, who lived on Doucette Avenue across from

Magnolia Elementary. "With her aggressive personality, [Babe] couldn't avoid getting into fights, and you know who always won—she did. She could swing those fists."

Though her neighborhood was segregated, Babe sometimes got into fistfights with African American kids, too. Her fists didn't discriminate. But she didn't see black kids very often. Blacks and whites went to separate schools. The Ku Klux Klan was powerful in Beaumont and worked to keep the races apart.

By the time she was ten, Babe "was the ringleader . . . the boss over us," Choate said. "She never worried about skinned knuckles and knees."

STRIKING OUT

Poppa built a gym in the backyard, believing his children should get plenty of exercise. He also had a different use for the broomstick than Momma had. With flatirons attached to either end, it became a weightlifting device for his sons. Babe cringed at the tablespoons of castor oil and black coffee Poppa spooned out to "keep your bowels clear." But she took full advantage of the gym equipment and would "get in there and work out with it too."

But Momma was determined that Babe would do her share of household chores. Babe's Saturday duty was scrubbing the linoleum floor along the side porch. Anything Babe did had to be fast or resemble a sport. The chore presented an opportunity: skating. Babe fastened brushes to her feet and "skate[d] around on the soap suds" until the baseball game started. Babe recalled, "[Momma would] take me by the ear and lead me over to it [the floor] and say 'Babe, look at that. Is that right?' . . . But I had to leave. The ball game was going to start."

The day Lillie graduated from elementary school changed Babe's attitude about her mother's strict ways. Laying out clothes for the family, Hannah remembered that she needed to buy the ground meat for supper. She asked Babe to go quickly and get some at Maniscalo's corner grocery store. On her way back, Babe saw a ball game in full swing at the Magnolia schoolyard. She couldn't resist playing. "A couple of minutes . . . stretched into an hour." By that time, a dog had polished off the meat Babe left on the lawn.

Supper was gone. Momma's sugar bowl—the place for saving money—was empty. The graduation party was ruined. Determined not to be a pest to Momma anymore, Babe decided to help out, since Momma and Poppa "had done so much for us seven Didrikson kids." But what could Babe do? She was only twelve years old.

Using the determination that helped her win ball games, Babe came up with a plan.

RACISM IN BEAUMONT

In the 1920s, life in Beaumont was segregated. That meant African Americans were prohibited by law to attend the same schools as whites or to shop at the same stores and eat at the same restaurants. Entire neighborhoods were divided by race and class. Beaumont's most powerful organization was the Ku Klux Klan, which by 1924 had more than three million members in the South and Midwest. The KKK claimed to uphold traditional values but used violence to intimidate and harm people, many of them African Americans.

The Beaumont KKK enforced its beliefs as guardians of "morality, Americanism, and racial purity." Members pistol-whipped, lashed, and tarred and feathered violators of their code. The Beaumont chapter also held public parades at Magnolia Park. The gatherings attracted thousands of onlookers, many of them children. Because of the Klan's intimidation, the National Association for the Advancement of Colored People closed its Beaumont chapter in 1924 and didn't reopen until 1930.

This Ku Klux Klan parade in downtown Beaumont was held on Armistice Day (Veterans Day) in 1922 and attracted fifty thousand onlookers.

BABE
VS.
THE GIRLS

"Before I was even into my teens, I knew exactly what I wanted to be. . . . My goal was to be the greatest athlete that ever lived."

—Babe Didrikson

"Inherent evils in interscholastic competition among girls demand its suppression."

—National Association of Secondary School Principals

When she was twelve, Babe worked in a factory like this one in Beaumont.

As a young girl, Babe stood out with her short bangs and denim skirt at a time when silky dresses and crimped curls were more popular.

The blisters on Babe's fingers began to bleed as she packed figs in a factory near Doucette Avenue. Playing baseball wouldn't bring the nine Didriksens money. Picking out bruised figs from the plump red ones did.

In 1923, there were few labor laws to limit where children worked or for how many hours. At age twelve, Babe worked eight to ten hours a week after school. She earned thirty cents an hour.

Babe knew she could do better. After a few days in the fig factory, she hatched a new plan. She convinced the owner of a gunnysack factory to hire her, sewing up sacks for potatoes—a penny a bag. Babe then asked him to bring her more sacks because she didn't want to wait when she finished.

It didn't matter that Babe's fingers were puffed up and raw. Momma had taught her how to make her own clothes, and Babe believed she could sew faster than anybody. "She was the best at *ever'thing* we did," Lillie said.

Babe was so good at sewing sacks that her boss let her slip out to play sports, "and then I'd work overtime and everything to make up for it."

For the first time, Babe had found a way to make money by being fast. She sewed sixty-eight sacks an hour, earning five or six dollars a week for Momma's sugar bowl. It was the same amount her oldest sister, Dora, paid her parents for room and board. The only coins Babe kept for herself went to buy a harmonica.

With no car or spare nickels to go see the movies—called the "flickers"—the Didriksens made their own entertainment. Evenings were spent on the front porch. The family sat on the steps below Poppa's "Old Glory" American flag. Momma sang and Poppa played the violin, accompanied by Babe on her brand-new harmonica and her brothers and sisters on drums and piano. Babe had learned to play harmonica by listening to Castor Oil Clarence, host of a popular radio show. The neighbors "came out on their own porches to listen." Those evenings were as special to Babe as playing ball in the sandlot.

TURNING FLIPS

One neighbor who heard the family play was Minnie Fisher. When "Aunt Minnie" wasn't living with her sister's family across the street from the Didriksens, she performed in a circus. She was one of the first "butterfly girls" or "iron jaw" performers in circus history, hanging sixty feet off the ground "suspended by her teeth and spinning at a terrific rate."

Minnie Fisher performed her iron-jaw act in circuses around the world. Minnie spun from her teeth like a "human aerial top," as seen in this 1898 Ringling Brothers photo (far right). Minnie also perfected a dangerous "slide for life" move, hanging by her teeth and rushing to the ground 250 feet below. Minnie introduced Babe to the circus life.

Babe was afraid to ride an elephant like this one during her brief time with the circus.

The routine drew gasps of amazement from the audience, but it was dangerous work. Also an equestrienne performer, Aunt Minnie once spent nearly a year in a full body cast after being thrown from a horse. Babe admired Aunt Minnie's daring independence. The circus was one of the few professions where a woman could earn money and fame with her physical talents.

Babe and Lillie wanted to be like Aunt Minnie. They put on union suits (long underwear) as make-believe circus outfits and swung from Momma's chinaberry tree in the backyard. The tree didn't survive. Luckily, Babe and Lillie did, despite falling "on our heads and everything."

The way Babe moved made Aunt Minnie believe she had talent. She wanted to take Babe with her to the circus. Performing in front of thousands of people and hearing applause for her athletic maneuvers sounded exciting to Babe. She had seen a circus in Beaumont, earning the price of admission by carrying water buckets to the animals.

Babe convinced her parents to let her go to California and train with the Morton Circus, if Lillie went, too. It was a huge step for two young girls who'd never been out of east Texas. The harrowing ride on zigzagging mountain roads to California in Aunt Minnie's car prepared them for the feats they'd have to accomplish at the training grounds.

Babe learned to hang by her toes, turn flips in the air, and walk a tightrope without an umbrella. She was also expected to ride an elephant. Babe looked up at the massive gray animal and hesitated. She took in a deep breath. Babe wasn't afraid of anyone or of heights or walking on a quarter-inch high wire. Suddenly, Babe realized she was afraid of elephants. Lillie was not. It was the only time Lillie had ever seen her sister "afraid of somethin' that I wasn't."

Mr. and Mrs. Didriksen missed their daughters. After several months, Poppa traveled by train to get them.

Back in Beaumont, Babe and Lillie enrolled in South End Junior High. They "didn't learn a thing" at the school they'd attended while in California, so they had to repeat a grade. Babe soon forgot about becoming a butterfly girl, but she'd learned how to capture an audience's attention.

TOO SMALL TO PLAY?

Babe dominated intramural sports at South End Junior High. Homeroom classes competed against each other, with softball and hardball the favorites. South End principal E. W. Jackson recalled that "the home room that had Babe in it always won any contest that was going on."

Babe captained the girls' baseball team, but most of her classmates didn't value sports as much as she did. The school ran contests for the cutest

Babe was the star of her junior-high-school baseball team. This photo appeared in the school's yearbook, **The Broadcaster,** *which referred to the group as "Mildred Didrikson's team." Physical-education teacher Ruby Gage said Babe kept a pair of dice in her pocket when she pitched and shook them for good luck.*

44

GIRLS' BASEBALL TEAM
Top Row, Left to right—Thelma Simpson, Evelyn Bridgewater, Velma Laxon, Phillis Sachitano, Ruby
Gage.
Second Row, left to right—Lois Blanchette, Coye Gillespie, Mary Revak, Ollie Dee Huckaby.
Bottom Row, left to right—Mildred Didrickson.

South Junior High Athletics

Athletics at South End Junior High School during the year of '25 and '26 has been very successful. Under the guidance of Mr. Edwin Smith, our coach, South End teams have always given a good account of themselves. The teams of '25 and '26 have always played good, clean, and fast games and have shown a spirit that only Mr. Smith can instill in his players and through the combination of this spirit and a true love for the cardinal and white have carried those same colors to glory with a clean record.

The first sport South End indulged in was football and in this we met with our first success, carrying off the Junior championship for the second successive year by defeating North End 13 to 7 in the final game of the season.

Our basketball team did not take the title but it won most of its games and came through the season with a really commendable record because of its determination, faithfulness, and fairplay.

Baseball furnished the chief attraction for the spring of the year and every thing considered we had a remarkable team. In spite of the rain we played a good many games, usually three or four a week. Baseball proved to be a school of experience in which every player learned some excellent lessons which will stay with him and benefit him for many days to come.

Now that the year is coming to a close every one's thoughts are turned to the future and we will live through the summer with the expectations that the coming year will be filled with more victories and greater successes than the one through which we have just passed.

and most popular students. (Unfortunately, they also chose the homeliest boy.) Photos of the winners were printed in the school yearbook, *The Broadcaster*. They took up more pages than the sports teams.

Fitting in was harder when Babe entered Beaumont High School. Beatrice Lytle, the school's first director of physical education for girls, was as tough as Babe and determined to assemble a winning girls' basketball team. She thought Babe was too small for the Miss Royal Purples squad.

Babe set out to prove "Coach Bea" wrong. She knew that she was good enough for the basketball team. She summoned the help of the boys' basketball and football coach, Lilburn "Bubba" Dimmitt. He helped Babe in between the practice drills he ran for the boys' team. Coach Dimmitt was impressed with Babe's skill and her confidence. Babe would remind Coach Dimmitt to "tell those women I can play basketball."

Babe practiced during her study halls, and it became obvious that her athletic achievements stood out from her academic ones. It was hard to convince Babe to read a book, though her English teacher, Ruth Scurlock, tried. She doubted that Babe would take the time to read anything unless it was a sports rule book.

Babe's excellence in sports soon changed Coach Lytle's mind about her size. Once Lytle saw Babe play, the coach was astounded by Babe's coordination and muscle memory. Lytle had no doubt that Babe "was blessed with a body that was perfect."

Babe and her high-school teammate and rival, Jackie Bridgewater, practice basketball.

As a freshman (the class that was known as the Fish), Babe starred on all the Royal Purple varsity teams, from basketball to tennis, baseball, and diving. Freshmen didn't usually make varsity teams. But Babe wasn't the only one to do so. Fellow freshman Evelyn "Jackie" Bridgewater was Babe's first female rival.

They didn't always get along, especially when they first met.

The Beaumont High School Miss Royal Purples never lost a game when Babe was in the lineup. Babe is in the front row, third from the left;

Jackie Bridgewater is in the front row, second from the right; and coach Bea Lytle is in the back row, first on the left.

Bridgewater said Babe challenged her, "and I went into my fighting stance and told her to come on." Babe mockingly called her Jack Dempsey—the heavyweight boxing champion of the time—"but [she] never closed in," Bridgewater said. "I never quit standing my ground with her. I could have whipped Babe."

The Royal Purples never lost a regular-season basketball game when Babe was on the team. At that time, girls played "three-court" basketball, with players being positioned in three zones. Unlike the men's game, in which players could run and dribble the length of the basketball court, girls could dribble just once and were not allowed to cross into a different zone. Those rules confined Babe, but with her long stride, she made the most of the zone near the basket. "With one dribble . . . and a jump she could sink the ball," said Lytle.

Babe's competitive nature made it difficult for her to make friends. The majority of girls at the high school didn't play sports. At Beaumont High, looks and appearance were important. Babe may not have had much use for books, but she had even less time for the girls who fussed with their clothing and wore lipstick. The *Pine Burr* yearbook printed large photos of students voted as "Favorites." Babe wasn't one of them.

Babe wore denim skirts, socks, and flat oxford shoes. The "society girls" curled their hair in permanent waves. They wore silk stockings and high heels. They were "sissy girls" in Babe's eyes, but they were the "overwhelming majority and they were the leaders," said Ruth Scurlock, who saw how difficult it was for Babe to fit in. "Even in her own tough neighborhood, the other girls didn't like her because she was an athlete."

Babe's high-scoring performances did mean something to the *Beaumont Journal* sports editor, Bill Scurlock, who was Ruth's husband. It wouldn't be long before Scurlock, who weighed 350 pounds and was nicknamed "Tiny," collected enough notes about Babe's achievements to fill a box.

HURDLING THE HEDGES

Seeing her name in the sports pages fueled Babe's ambition to continue winning. She cut out the reports and kept them. Babe had few friends besides Lillie, but she had a growing collection of clippings about her achievements.

In 1928, the sports section carried news about another event that caught Babe's attention: the Olympic Games in Amsterdam, the Netherlands. For the first time, women competed in Olympic track-and-field events. Babe was thrilled to finally read about women athletes, including American high-school student Betty Robinson, who won the 100-meter dash.

Babe and Poppa read the news of the Olympics together. The speed and power of the throwing, running, and jumping events intrigued her. The hurdles race combined speed and skill.

Babe was mesmerized. There wasn't a girls' track-and-field team at Beaumont High, but there were rows of hedges along Doucette Avenue on the same side as Babe's house.

When Babe wasn't leaping over the hedges on Doucette Avenue to prepare for the Olympic hurdles, she roller-skated to the corner store to get groceries for her family.

Babe figured they would be a good substitute for hurdles and could help in her training. She'd already decided that she wanted to be an Olympic champion.

Babe raced along the lawns on Doucette, clearing the hedges as she ran. But there was one that was higher than the others. Babe couldn't get over it and it interfered with her practices.

She knocked on the door of Oscar King. He owned the property with the higher hedge, three houses down from the Didriksens. Luckily, Babe had never broken one of his windows with a home run. Babe was persuasive. She convinced Mr. King to cut his hedge "down to where the rest of them were."

Babe hurdled the hedges, crooking her left knee to make it over the wide shrubs. Lillie ran beside her on the sidewalk. Babe soon overtook her sister.

It came as a surprise to Babe when she learned that the Olympics were held every four years. In her mind, she could take on the fastest women in the world right then and win.

In high school, track and field was still reserved for boys. The girls cheered them on. All the coaching Babe received was from Lillie and the hedges. Even though she triumphed in girls' sports, she wasn't being challenged enough.

Babe believed that if a girl "just goes in for games against girls when she is young, why she never gets used to being smashed around. Girls are nice to each other. Boys are rough with each other, and rougher with girls who crash into their game."

Babe hoped to play high-school football, but Texas rules did not allow girls in the game.

MANY ROADBLOCKS

But whether Babe wore her hair cropped like a boy or balked at wearing high heels, she was still a girl. All of the powerful people in her Texas city—politicians and business leaders—were men. Although it had been nearly ten years since women had earned the right to vote, women did not have the same rights as men. Since 1923, a group called the Women's Division of the National Amateur Athletic Federation (NAAF) had been trying to stop girls from competing in sports. Though Beaumont High School continued to support most girls' sports, the basketball season was cut short during Babe's junior year because of "growing aversity to interscholastic competition between girls." The National Association of Secondary School Principals stated that the "extremely strenuous physical and mental exertion and strain [of sports] are a menace to girls."

Even though Babe was as talented as the boys in some sports, she was not allowed to play on their high-school teams. On the Beaumont High School football field, as a senior, she proved that she had no equal when it came to kicking field goals. But being the best didn't matter: Babe was a girl.

Though Coach Dimmitt liked Babe and "let her try and kick some" in practice, there was no way the school board would let Babe in the football games. The Texas rules were "flat against letting a girl play a man's sport."

"Sports was a way of getting to be equal, and I think that's what carried Babe through and made her work so hard," said

Raymond Alford, who was captain of the football team. But Raymond could dream of playing professional baseball or football. That wasn't true for Babe.

Babe grew impatient. She wanted to compete against the best. The next Olympics were years away. She didn't enjoy schoolwork. There were no successful professional women athletes. What could Babe do?

A surprise meeting at a basketball game provided the answer.

BABE'S BIG BREAK

On February 5, 1930, Colonel Melvorne McCombs walked into a Houston high-school basketball game looking for a star to lead his semipro women's team. The top scorer with 19 points against Houston's Reagan High was the Miss Royal Purple standout—Babe Didrikson.

McCombs wanted Babe to play on his Dallas team. He also offered her a job as a typist. Babe was more than ready to leave the society girls and the snub from the football team. She quit school before graduation. Babe assured her parents she would return after the basketball season to finish.

Eleven days later, Babe played in her last high-school game. She left Coach Lytle and her team just a week before their championship game. The next night, Babe rode a train to Dallas. She'd accepted a job with McCombs's Employers

Casualty Company (ECC). It was difficult to leave her family, but Babe would be playing sports much of the time. She would also be making a good living that would help support her family.

Colonel McCombs bought train tickets for Poppa and Babe. Poppa would see that she arrived safely in Dallas. Babe brought along her harmonica and played into the night. The smell of Poppa's pipe tobacco from the lower bunk reminded Babe of times spent with her family in Beaumont.

BABE
VS.
THE BEST

"She was out for Babe, honey, just Babe. . . . She was not a team player, definitely not."

—Mrs. Reagan Glenn, Golden Cyclones basketball player

"It came time to announce my 'team.' I spurted out there all alone, waving my arms, and you never heard such a roar."

—Babe Didrikson, at the Women's National Track and Field Championships

Babe and her teammates won the national basketball title in 1931.

It was early morning when Babe and Poppa stepped off the train at Dallas Union Terminal. Colonel McCombs waited for them in his yellow Cadillac. Babe was eager to start her new life in Dallas. She wore her Sunday best: a blue silk dress she had sewn herself.

Melvorne Jackson McCombs was nicknamed "the Colonel" for his time in the military. He had been a track-and-field athlete in college, then coached high-school football.

McCombs managed the Employers Casualty Company's department for accident and cyclone insurance. But he spent most of his time recruiting and coaching the company's women's athletic teams. They were called the Golden Cyclones. Babe was impressed by his persuasive talk. Like Babe, McCombs knew how to get his way. He had helped Babe convince her parents to let her move to Dallas.

At the train station, McCombs signaled a porter to take Babe's suitcase. Tilting his Stetson hat, McCombs handed the man a quarter. Babe was stunned to see such a large tip "just for carrying those bags out." In February 1930, the nation was immersed in the Great Depression. People struggled to survive. Tens of thousands stood waiting in bread lines for something to eat, even in oil-rich towns like Beaumont.

McCombs knew Babe needed to work, since her family was poor and her father wasn't earning much money. Babe was hired to be a typist, earning $75 a month. The sum was more than her father or older siblings could bring in.

As the Colonel gave Babe a tour of the insurance company offices, she tried to impress him with her skill. Babe boasted that

As a typist for the Employers Casualty Company in Dallas, Babe was proud of how quickly her typing skills improved. At night and on weekends, she played for the company teams.

Babe is second from the right in the back row of this 1930 Employers Casualty basketball team photo.

she could type eighty-six words a minute, saying she'd won a contest at school for hitting the best speed.

It didn't matter to McCombs whether Babe knew how to type. She'd really been hired to help Employers Casualty win a national basketball title. They'd lost the championship game by one point the previous year to the Sunoco Oilers.

Babe would be playing basketball games at night and tournaments on weekends. In 1930, basketball was the most popular sport for women, and it brought attention to the companies that sponsored successful teams. McCombs knew Babe would be a star attraction. He'd "never . . . seen a man or a woman to compare with Babe Didrikson for natural ability."

The Women's Division of the NAAF blocked many high-school and college programs from the "prolonged and intense strain" of competition. But the organization couldn't prevent businesses and churches from forming leagues and competing for a national championship.

The "industrial leagues" were strongest in the South. Many of the best teams were in Dallas. The Women's Division opposed spectators at women's games and stressed "suitable costumes" for athletic activity, but McCombs ignored these restrictions. He'd made the Golden Cyclones one of the best teams by recruiting great athletes. McCombs gave them new uniforms with sleeveless tops and satin shorts, replacing the old-fashioned middy blouses and baggy bloomers that some teams still wore. The popular Cyclones drew up to four thousand spectators for their home games.

SIZING UP HER TEAM

Babe's new teammates waited for her in the office where they did clerical work, eager to meet the latest recruit. Babe had "never seen so many large girls—large feet, and large hands. They were really husky." The players weren't considered professional athletes because they did not get paid to play the games. They were paid to work. But it was clear why most of them had been hired. It was for their sports skills.

Babe would suit up that night and bump one of them from

This is to certify that _____

LOU HENRY HOOVER

Endorses the Platform of the Women's Division, National Amateur Athletic Federation

And is granted ____DONOR____ Membership

For one year from this 1st day of November, 19 35

Edith M. Gates
Chairman, Executive Committee

A ROADBLOCK FOR WOMEN

Not all women were pleased that girls were succeeding in athletics. The Women's Division of the National Amateur Athletic Federation was opposed to women and girls competing for sports championships. The group was founded in 1923 by Lou Henry Hoover, president of the Girl Scouts and wife of future U.S. president Herbert Hoover. It objected to the fact that girls' sports were being dominated by the best players, which they believed shut out other girls from participating.

The Women's Division began with a goal of promoting physical fitness. "A team for everyone and everyone on a team!" it stated. "This is the aim of the new plan for athletics among girls."

Mrs. Hoover was most interested in the physical benefits of exercise. But after she stepped down as president of the group, its mission quickly shifted to stopping girls and women from competing at all. It campaigned to eliminate out-of-school athletics, ticket sales for women's games, travel to sports events, and all publicity about women and girls in sports. It led a revolt against women's basketball and soon extended that effort to track and field.

The suppression was mostly felt in high schools and colleges, as industrial leagues and athletic clubs continued to grow.

Lou Henry Hoover enjoyed riding and camping and believed that girls and women should be physically fit. She was uncomfortable about the National Amateur Athletic Federation's stance against girls and women competing in sports, but she remained a lifetime member of the group.

the lineup. Lalia Warren asked Babe which position she was going to play. Babe "got a little pepped up" and asked Warren the same question. When Warren let Babe know she was the "star forward," Babe said, "Well, that's what I want to be." Though she was fresh out of high school, Babe made it clear that she wasn't intimidated by the stars on the team.

Babe had no time to practice with her teammates before that night's game and barely enough to alter her plaid basketball shorts. She sewed them skintight, the way she liked to wear them. Babe wasn't concerned about showing her legs. The new uniforms meant that nothing would slow down her play.

Dressed in a jersey with the number 7 that she'd worn since elementary school, Babe led the Cyclones to victory by scoring 14 points. Since the industrial leagues played two-court basketball, Babe had more room to maneuver and showcase her speed. She and the others were allowed to dribble as many times as they wanted.

The next day, Babe couldn't contain her excitement about the game and her new job. She sent a sloppy handwritten letter to *Beaumont Journal* sports editor Tiny Scurlock and enclosed a clipping about the game.

Dear Tiny: Played my first game last night the 18, and I never before practiced with them and they say that I was the the girl that that they have been looking for. They put me to [start] and kept me in until the finish.

Tiny I am a working girl and have got to get busy. Please keep this write up for me please or send it back when you get a chance. Thanks so much, Babe.

"KNOCKING THEM COLD"

Babe continued to lead the Cyclones to victories. Within two weeks, she had gone from being a high-school player to an industrial league sensation. Babe had shown that she belonged, competing (and starring) against the country's best women athletes.

Babe wrote to Tiny that she was "still knocking them cold" and with another prediction: "We have two . . . all-American forwards on our team and Mr. McCombs said that he would have three All American Forwards . . . before the season is over. . . . [I'll] get that All American Badge To put on my left sleeve of this hot orange sweater that I have."

The best players in the country were chosen as all-Americans. Babe was pleased that she'd impressed McCombs enough for him to consider her worthy of the title. Other companies took notice of Babe's play, too. Some of them tried to recruit her, including the Cyclones' main rival, the Sunoco Oilers. But Babe stayed loyal to Employers Casualty.

"I have a whole lots of fans now," Babe wrote to Tiny. "I have had two more offers. . . . The Sun Oil Man said that he could use me in the national this year but I am going to stay with the Golden Cyclones until this season is over."

Babe needed to share her sports accomplishments with someone who appreciated them. As a sportswriter, Tiny fit the bill. So she confided about her troubles and triumphs in her letters to him.

Babe focused on winning the national championship and not losing to the rival Sunoco Oilers again "if I can help it." She was also determined to take care of her family. Babe was only eighteen, but with Poppa out of work, she was now the family's main provider. Babe took the role seriously. It was a lonely time for her, being away from Lillie for the first time and missing her parents. But leaving home to play sports was an essential first step for Babe to have a career as an athlete.

Babe kept a small share of her $75-a-month salary for food and to pay her rent. She sent $45 of it home. "I wasn't spending anything on clothes," she said. "I had just the one pair of shoes, and the leather was beginning to curl." Babe didn't need much when it came to material things. She thrived on winning.

The only expensive item Babe bought was a new radio for her mother. Momma missed Babe; Lillie often noticed her mother crying. Babe couldn't wait to give the radio to Momma, and she held it on her lap during a train ride to Beaumont. She hoped Momma could listen to her basketball games and feel as if she was closer to Babe.

Babe shared an apartment with three teammates on Haines Avenue in Dallas. Her rent was $5 a month. She bought home-cooked breakfasts and dinners prepared by the wife of Cyclones assistant coach Danny Williams and looked forward to her pies edged with graham cracker crust. Other team members bought and ate their meals at the Williams home, too, but Babe never wrote to Tiny about making friends with the other players. They didn't like how Babe rarely passed the basketball, doing most of the scoring on her own.

The Cyclones advanced to the 1930 national championship tournament in Wichita, Kansas. Babe asked Lillie to join her on the trip for support. Still thinking of them as young girls, Momma insisted that Babe and Lillie wash their undergarments in "a little bitty sink" on the train and hang them out the window to dry overnight. By morning, the garments were blackened with soot. They had to rewash them and wear them wet.

Though her teammates resented Babe's ball hogging, they appreciated her winning ways. They could rely on Babe to make key shots, and she scored 210 points in five games during the tournament. In a close game against the Sunoco Oilers, the Cyclones picked Babe to take an important free throw. "You could choose anyone on your team to take the free throw," Babe said. "The other veteran players said to me, 'Here, you take it.' So I stepped up to the line, not thinking about it especially."

Babe missed the shot. In a repeat of the previous year's score, the Cyclones lost to the Oilers by one point (28–27). "I really felt bad about the whole thing," Babe said. McCombs and the Cyclones would have to wait another year for a chance at a national basketball championship.

A TURNING POINT

Babe had told her parents that she would return to school in June to graduate, but she had no intention of doing so. She kept working and played baseball and tennis for the company teams that spring. Her school records read "withdrew to play basketball."

One Saturday, McCombs brought Babe to Dallas's Lakeside Park to watch a track-and-field meet. Babe had never seen women compete in the sport and was eager to find out more. She knew about the sprints and the hurdles, but she asked McCombs about "this stick lying on the ground." It was a javelin, a spearlike metal rod that competitors threw.

Babe tried throwing it and "got pretty good distance, but it was so heavy—it was a men's javelin. . . . I slapped my back with it as I threw it, and raised a welt."

Babe then watched the hurdles and the broad jump, asking McCombs questions about technique and records. The day proved to be a turning point in Babe's athletic career. Track and field appealed to Babe because she could excel as an individual. She wouldn't have to rely on teammates to feed her the ball. But Employers Casualty no longer had a track-and-field team. Babe told McCombs that they should. By Monday afternoon, Babe also convinced the president of Employers Casualty and became captain of the team.

For Babe, the word "team" was a formality. "We all got together and started talking about this track team," she recalled. "One girl said, 'I'm going to throw the javelin.'

Another said, 'I'm going to throw the discus.' I said, 'Well, I'm going to do them all.' Everybody nearly died laughing."

Babe wasn't joking. The team's daily two-hour practices weren't enough for her. Babe trained after dinner, too, running up and down the hill on Haines Avenue, "jog [ging] my legs real high, and work[ing] my arms high, to get them in shape."

The evening before her first track-and-field meet, Babe worked late into the night to perfect her takeoff in the high jump and the broad jump. Then she pushed herself even further, sprinting a quarter mile around the track. By the time she reached the finish line, Babe was "seeing stars," and collapsed on the grass.

When McCombs heard about Babe's grueling routine, he grew concerned. "Her only fault," he said, "is that she unconsciously and unknowingly overtrains." McCombs worried that Babe had used up her strength at practice or, worse, that she would risk an injury that might sideline her for the basketball season. Babe proved him wrong.

The next afternoon, Babe and her team competed against several other teams at a track meet in Dallas. Babe won all four of the events she entered. "It was that last extra practice that did it," she said.

Babe was not satisfied with her high jump result. Her goal was to break the world record, but McCombs didn't think she could jump any higher unless she tried a different technique. To break the record, Babe would have to jump like a man.

The men's style, known as the Western roll, required more power. It was also risky. As Babe said, "Your feet had to cross the bar first. If your head went over first, then it was a 'dive' and didn't count." She would also be more likely to foul and more likely to injure herself with a rough landing. Would she have to give up the event?

Babe was willing to risk it. Learning the Western roll was frustrating and bruising. She fell. Hard. McCombs bribed her with milkshakes so she wouldn't give up. Then, just before the Texas state meet, Babe stepped on a shard of glass from a broken bottle and cut her foot. She visited a doctor twice to have it examined, and he "gouged around and made it so sore." Babe refused to bow out of the meet. Instead, she came within a half inch of the world record in the high jump. Her Western roll was working.

HIGHER GOALS

By the time Babe turned nineteen in June, she had sent enough press clippings to Tiny to fill a scrapbook. Babe felt less lonely now that she had a sport that was all her own. It had rekindled the excitement she'd felt when she and Poppa had read about the Olympics:

> *Oh! yeah! right after the track season I am gonna train for the Olympics in 1932. . . . at the National &*

HOMER R. MITCHELL, Pres. & Gen. Mgr.
A. F. ALLEN, Vice-President
L. W. GROVES, Vice-President & Secretary
E. E. WATTS, Vice-President & Treas.

W. B. HEAD, Chairman of the Board

A. H. PLYER, Asst. Sec'y & Asst. Treas.
L. A. GUTHRIE, Asst. Sec'y & Mgr. Claim Dept.
J. Y. MARTIN, Asst. Sec'y
M. J. McCOMBS, Mgr. Dept. of Safety

EMPLOYERS CASUALTY COMPANY

HOME OFFICE   DALLAS - TEXAS

June 8, 1930

Dear Tiny.-

Just got back from Shreveport from the Southern track meet
Well that makes that 13th gold medal that I have gotten. Made
me a braclet out of the first first ten that I got. and I got
3 from the Southern Meet. All gold and no silver. I am sending
you a write up from the times.

Why don't you drop me a line once in a while and tell me
about what you are going to do. Well Tiny I have got to go out
to the track field at S. M. U. and brush up for the Texas and
the National meet. So that I can Break a few worlds records

Tiny about that Fleshmens Yeast won't that Make me professional Well I don't wont to get that way right away. I
am gonna enter the tennis, swimming and every other kind of
meets over here and over there. get full of medals. You know
like ants . Well by and please send these writeups back
to me so that I can put them on the last page of my scrap book.
have you ever looked back at the old papers and found the
write ups that you said you were going to get, I left a place
blank for them and as soon as they come I will fix it up.

Am training plenty hard but thats the only way to make them
struggle and then for the competition.

Some typest Huh?

Just Babe.

Babe wrote letters to Beaumont Journal *sports editor Bill "Tiny"
Scurlock. They became lifelong friends. Babe's notes to Tiny were
a gushing mix of accomplishments and schemes. They were also
filled with misspellings. Tiny kept his own notes about Babe: "Her
favorite color is blue. She likes chicken legs and fish in a big way,"
Scurlock wrote. "She always had a harmonica stuck in her jeans."*

Olimpic gonna sho [everyone I] have ants in my pants.
By—Babe. P.S. Please send these write up[s] to
my mama.

Babe made the 1930 national championship meet her next target. The event was right in her backyard of Dallas. The competition would be the toughest Babe had ever faced. She'd be up against Cleveland's Stella Walsh, who was a world record holder.

Babe and Walsh brought out the best in each other. In the broad jump, Walsh broke the world record on her first attempt. Babe followed by jumping farther. With each jump, they continued to outdo each other. "Babe broke the world record five times and I had to break it right back again six times in order to beat her," Walsh said.

Babe admired Walsh and treated her with more respect than she did most of her competitors. Babe admitted that Walsh was the better jumper that day and "took first place away from me by jumping a quarter of an inch farther." Babe set two world records in winning the javelin and the baseball throw. She had been competing in track and field only for a few months, but Babe was already proving to be one of the best in the world.

Babe's success carried over to the 1931 basketball season. She led the Golden Cyclones to their first national basketball title. Babe was the star of the tournament and hit a late shot to beat the Wichita Thurstons.

Before Babe, Stella Walsh was the leading "feminine track star" and the fastest woman on earth. Walsh competed in the sprints, discus, and the broad jump. Born in Poland and raised in Cleveland, Ohio, Walsh represented Poland in the 1932 Olympic Games, winning the 100-meter sprint. Like Babe, Walsh challenged society's image of femininity. She set many world records during her lengthy career in track and field. Tragically, she was killed at age sixty-nine when she tried to defend herself during a robbery and was shot. An autopsy discovered the surprising fact that Walsh had male and female sex organs. She lived her life as a woman.

Babe (middle row, second from right) led the 1931 Employers Casualty basketball team to the national title.

Waiting for a basketball game to begin, Babe sits with Colonel Melvorne McCombs to her right and Employers Casualty team chaperone Mrs. Henry Wood to her left.

LOSING FOCUS

As Babe's success grew, her relationship with McCombs changed. She needed McCombs but believed that he needed her even more. Babe knew how valuable she was to Employers Casualty. Her high-school coach, Bea Lytle, thought the company "exploited [Babe] for their own advertising" but that Babe "could never have achieved the fame and fortune that she had had she not connected up with a group that was interested in, in athletics."

More recruitment letters rolled in from companies wanting Babe to join their teams. But Babe had signed a contract to remain a Golden Cyclone for another year, earning $90 a month. Even so, having a well-paying job during the hard times of the Depression no longer satisfied Babe. She believed she was being taken advantage of because her athletic skills brought Employers Casualty headlines and even more fans.

Babe also wanted more money because her family kept asking for it. "Babe's family . . . always had their hands out to her," said Ruth Scurlock. "She was still practically a child making a pittance pay. . . . She never had as much money as they thought she did, but they wanted her to give, give, give."

Babe asked McCombs for more money.

McCombs refused. Babe had finally met her match when it came to being stubborn. Instead of more money, the company provided her with free golf lessons at the Dallas Country Club, and they "are plenty nice so they won't have to raise my pay."

But Babe wouldn't take no for an answer. She hatched

another plan, this one more shocking than her schemes as a child on Doucette Avenue. What Babe proposed must have come as a surprise to Tiny Scurlock. Babe tried to get him involved in a plan to deceive her employer.

> *Write me a letter telling me of a better job that I can get and more money[—]about $125.00 a month. . . . This is just to make them break a loose and pay me a little more dough. Put the price and everything make a keen contract form and make it plenty real. Tiny don't tell anyone about this will you, because I couldn't have it get to Dallas. . . . So Tiny will you please do that for me Write me just as though I had never written to you—so they won't suspect. Love Babe Didrikson*

Tiny did not write a fake contract, and there was no more mention of the scheme. Babe had other problems to deal with. Her "me first" attitude made Babe an outstanding track athlete, but it clashed with her teammates on the basketball court. It didn't help that the team was now known in the newspapers as "Babe and her Employers Casualty Girls."

"I admit I admired Babe because of all the things she could do," said Babe's teammate Mrs. Reagan Glenn. "But some of the other gals really resented her. . . . She was out for Babe, honey, just Babe."

Her teammates' rejections stung. Babe wrote to Tiny about it.

But she was unwilling to admit that the snubs were hurtful or that she was part of the problem. Babe described the friction another way:

> *Dearest Tiny—Heck I'm tired of this old Burg. . . .*
> *These girls here are just like they were in Beaumont*
> *High School Jealous and more so because they are all*
> *here and trying to beat me. But they can't do it. . . .*
> *Let's get into some action and try and get me out of*
> *this place. And then maybe someday I'll come back*
> *then and whip the socks off the whole darn bunch. . . .*
> *I remain, Yours very truly, Babe Didrikson.*

With no friends in Dallas, Babe spent her lunch breaks alone at a drugstore soda fountain. For a treat, she ate toasted cupcakes washed down with a Coke. The boy who served the food was a basketball fan and went to the games. Sometimes he gave Babe an extra Coke for free.

During the 1932 basketball season, Babe often sat on the bench and sulked about her salary and her teammates. "I [won't] try to play ball," she wrote. But Babe's competitive drive was stronger than her combative nature, and that drive finally kicked in during the national tournament. Babe helped the Golden Cyclones make it to the championship game, where they finished as runners-up. Babe was named an all-American for the third year in a row. Then she got ready for the new track season.

AIMING FOR THE GAMES

The 1932 U.S. Track and Field Championships in Evanston, Illinois, doubled as the qualifier for the Olympic Games. The top three finishers in most events would earn a place on the U.S. Olympic Team. Babe was expected to qualify. But when McCombs refused to let her take an extra week's vacation, Babe quit Employers Casualty a month before the critical meet.

Babe headed back to Beaumont. Suddenly, on the train ride home, Babe knew she'd made a mistake. How would she support her family or compete for a spot on the Olympic team if she no longer worked for Employers Casualty? The next day, Babe returned to Dallas in tears and apologized to McCombs.

McCombs welcomed her back. He'd crafted a spectacular plan of his own that would bring more publicity to Employers Casualty than any national basketball championship. Shutting out the other teammates who wanted a chance to qualify for the Olympics, McCombs put Babe in the spotlight. Convinced she could win the entire meet on her own, he made Babe the only member of the ECC track-and-field team. Babe would compete in eight events at the Olympic trials as a "one-girl track team."

Babe traveled to Evanston with Mrs. Henry Wood, the official chaperone of the Golden Cyclones. She accompanied the team on all of their trips.

On July 15, the night before the meet, Babe experienced

violent stomach pains. When she put her hand on her stomach, it "would just bounce up and down." Mrs. Wood called the hotel doctor. He diagnosed the malady as "nerves."

After a restless night, Babe and Mrs. Wood overslept. Frantic to hail a cab and make it to the stadium on time, Mrs. Wood told Babe to change into her bright orange uniform in the cab. She held a blanket around Babe for cover.

By the time the meet started, the temperature in Evanston soared past one hundred degrees. Other competitors soothed their nerves and sweating bodies by sitting on a block of ice. Babe arrived at Northwestern University's Dyche Stadium just in time. The spectators cheered as the Employers Casualty "team" was announced. "You never heard such a roar," Babe said. "It brought out goose bumps all over me."

Babe's competitors weren't roaring; they were fuming. "We suddenly heard that they were going to let Babe compete in as many events as she wanted," said hurdler Evelyne Hall. "We were mad because we had always been limited to three events. . . . [Babe] was eliminating other girls from a chance for an Olympic berth."

Hall's team, the Illinois Women's Athletic Club, had captured the national title the previous three years. Hall won the hurdles in 1929 and 1930, but finished second to Babe in 1931.

The *Dallas News* had written that "while last year entrants were limited to three events . . . the field is wide open this year." At least it was for Babe. Babe hadn't set out to break the rules.

She just didn't think any competitor should be limited to a specific number of events if she was good enough to compete in them all. Athletes like Hall spent most of their efforts perfecting one event. Babe practiced for eight of them.

Despite having little sleep the night before, Babe was primed to perform. She raced from event to event, breaking her own world records in the baseball throw and the javelin. She won the broad jump and the shot put, placed fourth in the discus, and competed in the 100-meter dash. Babe was scoring more points by herself than all of the other teams.

"It was one of those days in an athlete's life when you know you're just right," Babe said. "You feel you could fly. You're like a feather floating in air."

Babe qualified for the final in the 80-meter hurdles, where she faced Evelyne Hall. The race was extremely close. "The judges huddled at the finish line and we crowded around," said Hall, who was certain that she had won. Finally, the judges announced that Babe had finished first.

Babe rushed to her last event: the high jump. As the bar rose higher, the competition came down to just Babe and the Philadelphia Meadowbrook Club's standout jumper, Jean Shiley. At the age of sixteen, Shiley had finished fourth in the 1928 Olympics. Shiley (who was 5 feet 9 inches tall) and Babe (who was 5 feet 6) tied for first, clearing 5 feet 3³/₁₆ inches—a new world record.

By the end of the day, Babe had won five events, tied for

first in another, and smashed three world records. As McCombs predicted, she won the meet single-handedly with 30 points. Hall's Illinois team—with twenty-two competitors—finished second.

Only three of the events Babe won were on the Olympic schedule. She hadn't taken a spot from another competitor, but she'd shattered the Women's Division's belief that "under prolonged and intense strain [in competition] a girl goes to pieces nervously." Babe may have been nervous, but she broke records anyway. Babe had fulfilled the goal she'd set four years earlier, hurdling the hedges on Doucette. She was an Olympian.

In less than three hours, Babe had carved a place in history, establishing herself as the greatest woman athlete not only of that day, but of all time. Sportswriters knew it. "The most amazing series of performances ever accomplished by any individual, male or female, in track and field history," United Press reporter George Kirksey wrote. Others filled their columns with praise about Babe's achievements on a day that the track-and-field world would never forget.

Kirksey ended his article by writing that Babe would lead the American women's Olympic track-and-field team in Los Angeles. "Such assistance as she may need against the foreign invasion will be provided by fifteen other young ladies."

Babe's main opponents at the Olympic Games wouldn't be the rest of the world; they would be her teammates and, soon after, some of the American sportswriters.

Babe leaps to victory in the broad jump at the 1931 U.S. Track and Field Championships. She also won the baseball throw and the 80-meter hurdles in that meet.

WOMEN IN THE OLYMPICS

French aristocrat Baron Pierre de Coubertin believed sport could transform men into gentlemen. In the 1890s, Coubertin focused on reviving the Olympic Games. He believed that a sports festival, like those held in ancient Greece, could help solve worldwide problems. He founded the International Olympic Committee (IOC) and spent his family fortune to bring back the Games.

Like the ancient Games, Coubertin's version left no room for women to participate. Only men took part in the first modern Olympics in 1896. Women did compete in the 1900 Games, participating on mostly male teams in equestrian, sailing, and croquet. Two events were reserved for women only: lawn tennis and golf.

Women's swimming and diving were added in 1912, but track and field did not receive the same acceptance. Considered a masculine sport for the working class, track and field, and its grittiness, was reserved solely for men.

Baron Pierre de Coubertin founded the International Olympic Committee, but he believed that women should have no part in the Games.

Furious that the IOC refused to include women's track and field, French athlete Madame Alice Milliat created the International Women's Sports Federation. The organization staged the Women's Olympic Games in 1922. The event included sixty-five athletes from five countries. Twenty thousand spectators cheered competitors in track-and-field events.

Angry that Milliat used the Olympic name, IOC officials changed their stance about admitting women's track and field. They added the sport to the 1928 Games, but only on an experimental basis. After some women struggled to finish the 800-meter race, the race was dropped from Olympic competition and didn't return until 1960.

Coubertin resigned as IOC president in 1925. He never altered his stance on women's participation in the Olympics. "As to the admission of women to the Games," Coubertin stated, "I remain strongly against it." At his request, Coubertin's heart was removed after he died in 1937, and it was buried at Olympia in Greece, site of the male-only ancient Olympic Games.

Tennis star Helen Wills Moody won two gold medals in the 1924 Olympics (singles and doubles matches) during a time when women's participation in the Games was limited. Moody was an intense competitor like Babe, but she mostly ignored her opponents. Sportswriter Grantland Rice referred to her as "Little Miss Poker Face."

No. 7119

Xth OLYMPIAD - LOS ANGELES - 1932

Identity Card

Valid 120 Days From Date of Entry Into the United States of America.

NAME _Didrikson Mildred_
           (Surname)   (Given names)

DATE & PLACE OF BIRTH _June 26, 1913_
Port Arthur, Tex

DOMICILE
- Street
- City
- Country _U. S. A._

NATIONALITY _American_

Issued by the Xth Olympiade Committee of the Games of Los Angeles, U. S. A., 1932, Ltd. at Los Angeles, California,

January 25th, 1932

President   General Secretary

Babe intentionally listed the wrong year of birth on her Olympic identification card. She was born in 1911, not 1913.

BABE
VS.
HER TEAM

"I came out here to beat everybody in sight, and that is what I am going to do."

—Babe Didrikson

"If there is anything more dreadful aesthetically or more depressing than the fatigue-distorted face of a girl runner at the finish line, I have never seen it."

—Paul Gallico, sportswriter

Chicago's Union Station, about 1912

The train at Chicago's Union Station carried a red, white, and blue banner: U.S. OLYMPIC TEAM. Babe didn't need a banner to announce her presence. She leaped on a bicycle near the train and "started beating her chest and screaming at the top of her lungs: 'Did you ever hear of Babe Didrikson? If you haven't you will!'" said Evelyne Hall.

Now that she was a world-class champion, Babe saw no reason to change her confrontational attitude. Babe boarded the Olympic train for Los Angeles more confident than ever.

Based on her outstanding day in Evanston, sportswriters predicted Babe would be the "teenage" star of the Olympics. They believed Babe was nineteen, but she was twenty-one years old. Babe had lied about her age. She'd marked the birth year "1913" on her Olympic identification card. Babe changed the year to appear younger. She thought being a teenager would make her achievements even more impressive.

The five-day train trip to Los Angeles gave the women track-and-field athletes time to get to know each other. Even confined to a train, Babe focused on getting in better shape. "Most of the girls sat around watching the scenery and playing cards and gabbing," Babe said. "I was busy taking exercises and doing my hurdle bends and stuff. . . . Several times a day I'd jog the whole length of the train and back. People in the other cars took to calling out, 'Here she comes again!'"

Babe's energy and ego made it "impossible to get to know her," said high jump rival Jean Shiley. "[Babe] was always chattering, talking, bragging. There was never a chance for a dialogue."

Babe did try to make friends in the only way she knew how—with practical jokes like the ones she had pulled on the kids back in Beaumont. Babe thought the antics were funny. Most of her teammates found them annoying, except for javelin thrower Gloria Russell. She joined in the fun.

"They especially liked to throw [pillows] at girls who wouldn't retaliate," said Hall. "The pillows would get caught on the hooks attached to the berths; they'd split open and we had feathers all over the car."

It was a long journey for the rest of the team, dodging pillows and ice-cube showers courtesy of Babe. She blasted her harmonica at anyone who tried to ignore her.

On the train, the team decided who would be the captain. Babe believed that the best athlete should be chosen, but the others voted against her. "If Babe had won, the team would have been simply torn apart," said Shiley, who was elected captain.

Babe shrugged off the rejection. She kept working out on the train.

The 1932 Games were only the second time women competed in track and field at the Olympics. Babe had qualified for the javelin, high jump, and 80-meter hurdles. She hoped to add another event. Having competed in eight events at the trials, Babe didn't see any reason to limit her competition to just three.

"ELEVEN WRETCHED WOMEN"

Babe was driven to win as many gold medals as she could. She symbolized everything that the Women's Division of the NAAF was against. The group had petitioned to have women's track and field eliminated from the Olympics. They pointed to the 1928 Olympic Games in Amsterdam and reports of the sweaty collapse of "eleven wretched women" following the 800-meter race. It didn't matter that the reports were untrue. (Only one woman actually fell while battling to a close finish.)

The Women's Division had proposed an alternative "showcase" that would be "for the opportunity of putting on in Los Angeles during the Games (not as part of the Olympic program) a festival which might include singing, dancing, music," and other exhibitions. The group succeeded in preventing the 800-meter race from taking place in the 1932 Olympics, but they couldn't stop Babe and other women from competing in the other events.

But another powerful movement was gaining momentum in Los Angeles. This one supported the women athletes. Hollywood's most famous movie stars spoke out in their favor. The actress Mary Pickford took to the radio airwaves, inviting women to the Olympics to watch the female athletes do great things. "While their records have not yet equalled the men's," Pickford announced, "notice, I say 'not yet'—they have accomplished wonders in the short time in which they have been competing."

Sportswriters covering the Olympics—most of them men—questioned whether women should compete in track and field. They saw it as a male sport and wanted to keep it that way. Westbrook Pegler of the *Chicago Tribune* wrote that the men thought it best if women competed in the more socially acceptable swimming and fancy diving events, believing a "woman's place in the Olympic meets is in the water, not on land." He said women should be "prevented from cluttering up the lot with delicate parodies of the mighty feats that males perform."

Grantland Rice, the most famous sportswriter of the day, disagreed. He was eager to watch Babe and the others compete. He knew that "male athletes and most male coaches won't take the feminine side of the Olympic Games any too seriously." Rice was unsure how Babe would do but thought that women track athletes would "provide a refreshing variety, even if they don't come close to male marks."

Babe was eager to make her presence known even before

Stars of all types gathered for this photo at the 1932 Olympics. From left are swimmer Helene Madison, sportswriter Grantland Rice, Babe Didrikson, actor Will Rogers, diver Georgia Coleman, and sportswriter Braven Dyer.

she stepped on the track. As soon as the train reached Los Angeles, she proclaimed, "I came out here to beat everybody in sight, and that is what I am going to do."

BOLD PREDICTIONS

Babe let it be known that she wanted to enter four events, despite the Olympic rules. "What I want to do most of all . . . is to win four firsts—something no girl has ever done," Babe said. "If they will let me enter the discus throw, . . . I think I can do it."

Babe hoped to replace Ruth Osburn, who had won the discus in Evanston. Osburn was nursing a sore arm from a car accident. Babe kept pressing her about how she was feeling. Babe had finished fourth in the discus at the trials. She felt she'd be next in line to replace Osburn if she was unable to throw.

Still stinging from the lopsided arrangement that had allowed Babe to perform in so many events at the trials, Babe's teammates opposed her four-event Olympic plan. "To set it aside," two-time Olympian Lillian Copeland said, "even for an athletic prodigy such as Babe Didrikson—is unwise in my mind. The rule should be enforced."

The women stayed at the Chapman Park Hotel. The new Olympic Village had been built for men only. Babe shared an apartment-style suite with two teammates: sprinter Mary Carew and Ruth Osburn, the woman Babe hoped would drop out of the discus event.

The roommates' opinions of Babe couldn't have been more different. "You see people you dislike," Osburn said, "but you try to stay away from them."

Carew liked Babe and was inspired by her. Babe helped the sprinter overcome a lack of confidence. "Here I was in with [Babe] who gave me courage. . . . She was awfully good to me," Carew said. "She would say, 'Hey, kid, get out there, you're as good [as] they are.'"

CELEBRITY TREATMENT

Sportswriters weren't the only reporters wanting to interview Babe. Hollywood gossip columnists roamed the lobby of the Chapman Park Hotel. They recorded the comings and goings of the women athletes as if they were motion-picture starlets. Babe's domineering nature fascinated the reporters. She had the confidence of a male athlete. It was a sharp contrast to the shy, delicate girls who competed in the water events.

Columnists asked about such things as her beauty, diet, and sewing. "The greatest girl athlete in the world just now, with a special liking for men's games, is as feminine as hairpins," one gossip columnist wrote. Others noted that Babe was as athletic as a man, but they needed assurance that she also liked womanly things. Babe told them that she didn't have time for romance. "Athletics are all I care for," she said. "I sleep them, eat them, talk them, and try my level best to do them as they should be done. You've got to feel that way."

Celebrities wanted to meet "the greatest girl athlete," too. Track-and-field practices were held in the mornings, but afternoons were spent at luncheons hosted by movie studios and the most famous movie actors of the day. These events were captured in newspapers for the world to read or talked about on the radio. Columnists and broadcasters interviewed Babe as often as they could.

Though she said she had no time for romance, Babe did want to meet actor Clark Gable. "So you're the big shot all the sissies are raving about," she told him. And the famous transatlantic pilot Amelia Earhart thought Babe's stardom could publicize an upcoming flight. Earhart tried to convince Babe to come along. Babe declined.

Hollywood—the movie capital of the world—caught Olympic fever, and the excitement spread across the nation. Americans were eager to take a break from the doom and gloom of the economy. They were especially ripe for an athlete like Babe Didrikson. Though many white-collar (or office) workers were unemployed, the Depression was felt deepest by blue-collar (or factory) workers and farmers. These American workers longed to follow a winner who had come from hard times and triumphed through the visible sweat of her labor. They loved how Babe spoke in plain terms. She was one of them.

"Folks say that I go about winning these athletic games because I have the cooperation thing that has to do with eye, mind and muscle," Babe said in her slow Texas drawl. "That sure is a powerful lot of language to use about a girl from Texas, maybe they are right about it. All I know is that I can run and I can jump and I can toss things and when they fire a gun or tell me to get busy I just say to myself, 'Well, kid, here's where you've got to win another.'"

Within a few days, Babe would try "to win another" on the biggest stage she had faced so far in her career. Track and field needed to be a success at the Los Angeles Olympic Games to put the problems of the 1928 Olympics to rest. Babe had to back up her boasting.

Babe does some target shooting with Amelia Earhart, the famous pilot. Earhart tried to convince Babe to fly with her, but Babe said no.

BABE'S BEST FOES

Babe roared into the 1932 Olympic Games on a wave of stardom, but her teammates arrived with far less publicity. Babe had much in common with her toughest competitors in the high jump and the hurdles. As kids, they hadn't conformed to the usual roles of girls. And they grew up to be serious athletes.

JEAN SHILEY

Like Babe, Jean Shiley had been a tomboy as a kid, scurrying around her neighborhood in Havertown, Pennsylvania, to keep up with her three brothers. She played football with them, climbed trees, and delighted in turning cartwheels and doing handstands.

In high school, Shiley excelled on the tennis, field hockey, and track-and-field teams. She was a force on the basketball team, too, demonstrating the jumping ability that would lead her to Olympic success. She was fortunate to practice high jumping some days at the University of Pennsylvania's Franklin Field. On other days, she trained at home by jumping over a fishing pole balanced between two clothesline supports.

Shiley earned a spot on the U.S. Olympic team and placed

fourth in the high jump during the 1928 Olympic Games. To pay for her college education, she took a job as a salesgirl at Wanamaker's department store in Philadelphia. Wanamaker's sponsored a track-and-field team called the Meadowbrook Club. Shiley competed for the club.

Babe and Jean Shiley were friendly but competitive rivals in the high jump.

EVELYNE HALL

As a girl, Evelyne Hall had a mischievous streak like Babe's. "I really was a daredevil," she said. "We lived near a railroad switching yard and, believe it or not, I used to hop on the ladders of the boxcars and ride into the switching yard."

Hall loved to compete, too, spending many of her Saturdays at the local Jewish People's Institute in Chicago. "I think the greatest thrill was running the relays," she said. Hall also enjoyed "those long ropes hanging from the ceiling, which we could climb up and down."

Evelyne married a telephone company worker named Leonard Hall in 1927. Leonard was a pole vaulter and broad jumper, and he coached Evelyne and traveled with her to meets. She was the national hurdles champion in 1929 and 1930. After she lost a close race to Babe at the 1931 national championships in Jersey City, she and Leonard worked for an entire year to perfect her form to take on Babe in the 1932 national meet.

Evelyne Hall is second from the left in this photo of the 1931 national championships. Babe (at right) set a world record when she won the 80-meter hurdles.

BABE
vs.
THE WORLD

"Didrikson leaps the hurdles . . . and runs on the flat like a scared coyote."

—Damon Runyon, sportswriter

"Win the next event? Well, I hope so. That's what I'm here for."

—Babe Didrikson

Babe runs the 80-meter hurdles at the 1932 Olympics.

Babe had never seen so many people. Spectators crowded into the Los Angeles Coliseum on the warm and sunny Saturday afternoon of July 30. The stadium boasted 105,000 seats. All of them were filled for the Olympics' opening ceremonies. Men fanned their faces with straw boater hats.

The 50,000 people who didn't get tickets or couldn't afford the two-dollar admission price mingled outside. Thousands more picnicked on the lawn. With vendors set up on the sidewalks and flags flying above the rim of the stadium, the day took on a carnival atmosphere.

When Babe and the other American athletes marched onto the track as the representatives of the final country to do so, even the movie stars watching in their fenced-off area became mere fans. "Just for once," the *Los Angeles Times* reported, "being a world-famous motion picture star was of no consequence whatever."

THE Xth OLYMPIAD

OPENING DAY AT THE LOS ANGELES OLYMPIC STADIUM, JULY 30, 1932

Nearly two thousand athletes from thirty-seven countries gathered in the Los Angeles Coliseum for the opening ceremonies of the 1932 Olympic Games and took the Olympic Oath. More than one hundred thousand spectators cheered, and a thousand-member choir sang "The Star-Spangled Banner."

Babe arrived at the Olympic Games ready "to beat everybody in sight."

Reporters wrote that the event took on a holy feeling as thousands of pigeons were released into the air and athletes recited the Olympic Oath in several languages.

Roasting in the heat and wearing a bell-shaped hat to complement her white uniform and red vest, Babe could only think about her feet. "I couldn't enjoy the ceremonies much after we got out there," she remembered. "We all had to wear special dresses and stockings and white shoes. . . . I believe that was about the first time I'd ever worn a pair of stockings in my life. . . . As for those shoes, they were really hurting my feet."

Babe kicked off her buckskin shoes to avoid blisters. She'd be competing the next day in the first of her three events, the javelin. She'd been told by the women's track-and-field coach, George Vreeland, that she would have to stick to the Olympic limit of three. (The women's javelin was making its Olympic debut; it replaced the controversial 800-meter race.)

Missing from the opening ceremonies was the U.S. president, Herbert Hoover. Many people blamed Hoover for the nation's difficult financial times. Across America, homeless people set up tents and built shelters nicknamed "Hoovervilles." Unable to afford gasoline to get their cars going, some travelers strapped their automobiles to horses, calling them Hoover wagons.

Hoover chose not to attend the Olympic ceremonies, leaving Vice President Charles Curtis to open the Games. It was the first time that a host country's head of state did not preside over an Olympics. Despite the country's troubles, complaining took

THE HOOVERVILLE OLYMPICS

By 1932, with the United States in its third full year of the Great Depression, Americans were fed up with President Herbert Hoover. The closest the president got to the Olympics was when he took a bite of a ceremonial loaf of bread he'd been sent that had also been served to Olympic athletes.

The day before the Olympics' opening ceremonies, Hoover was holed up in the White House after a night of deadly rioting outside. Thousands of World War I veterans had camped out nearby, demanding their army bonuses early. Acting swiftly, General Douglas MacArthur (who had been the American Olympic Committee president in 1928) commanded 1,500 soldiers as they marched up Pennsylvania Avenue near the White House "completely equipped for battle." Major George S. Patton (who had been an Olympian in the pentathlon in 1912) followed with six battle tanks, ordering the cavalry to charge. It was the first time troops had been called to the capital since the War of 1812.

Despite predictions that the poor economy would doom the Olympics, Los Angeles "blossomed out in a brilliant burst" and "stores and hotels looked like old times." The 1932 Olympics were the first to turn a profit—to the sum of one million dollars.

Nearly twenty thousand World War I veterans marched on Washington, D.C., in 1932, demanding their bonuses and chanting "Here we stay 'til the bonus they pay." The veterans had been camped on the National Mall for six weeks until the U.S. Army destroyed the camp on July 28.

a backseat to the Games. Many Americans pulled out what little change they had in their pockets and doled out the two bucks for admission. Empty, inside-out pockets were called "Hoover flags" to mock the president.

Babe's younger brother, Bubba, couldn't afford the trip to watch his sister compete. Instead, he hitchhiked part of the way from Texas and hoboed it to Los Angeles by illegally hopping onto trains. Bubba was picked up by authorities in Oklahoma and detained. Babe didn't know where he was and grew worried.

"LIKE A CATCHER'S PEG"

The weather was much different the day after the opening ceremonies. As Babe warmed up for the javelin throw, "shadows were coming up over the stadium, and it was turning pretty cool." More than sixty thousand spectators gathered for the competition.

The first time Babe threw the javelin during the warm-up, she nearly pierced the leg of a German competitor. Rattled and concerned about the danger of continuing, Babe stopped her warm-up and hoped for the best.

In the distance, Babe spotted a tiny German flag in the lawn. It signified the mark of 132 feet 7/8 inches that Ellen Braumüller had achieved in winning gold at the 1930 Women's World Games. It was listed in the Olympic program as the world record. (Babe's longer throw from the Olympic trials hadn't been officially recognized yet.) Braumüller was favored to win and was warming up nearby.

When the competition began, Babe was the first to throw. Her high-school physical education teacher, Bea Lytle, had made the trek from Texas and watched in the stands. Taking her mark, Babe jogged, then stutter-stepped down the sandy runway, the javelin resting on her right shoulder. When she got to the foul line, she stood on her toes, ready to let the javelin soar. Her hand slipped, but Babe quickly held the javelin firm and let it fly before she spun around.

A sharp pain shot through Babe's shoulder as the javelin sailed into the air. The throw was an unusual one and not the way Babe intended. "My hand slipped off the cord on the handle," she said. "Instead of arching the way it usually did, that javelin went out there like a catcher's peg from home plate to second base. It looked like it was going to go right through the flag."

The javelin kept going, slicing the air on a journey past Braumüller's world mark. It pierced the ground more than 11 feet beyond the record. When Babe's distance was announced—143 feet 4 inches—the crowd roared. Babe had set a new world record.

The record came at a price. "Nobody knew it, but I tore a cartilage in my right shoulder when my hand slipped making that throw," Babe said. "On my last two turns, people thought I wasn't trying, because the throws weren't much good. But they didn't have to be."

Babe practices with the javelin shortly before winning the Olympic event.

No one could throw anywhere near Babe's mark that afternoon. Braumüller settled for silver. Babe's prankish teammate, Gloria Russell, finished sixth.

"A woman athlete [has stolen] the honors of the day from the men," wrote *New York Times* columnist Arthur Daley. From that point on, spectators and writers flocked to watch Babe's events. They were eager to see if she could back up her brash predictions.

Babe didn't complain about her injured shoulder. She'd just won her first gold medal and the first women's gold medal of the Olympic Games for the U.S. team. But Babe still had two more events that she planned on winning.

CLOSEST RACE EVER

Babe prepared for the qualifying round of the hurdles to be held in four days. Coach Vreeland expressed concern about Babe's unconventional hurdling style, which she'd developed while jumping the hedges on Doucette Avenue. Vreeland wasn't happy about Babe's "refusing to take any new instruction from him."

Vreeland didn't have to worry. Using the peculiar form that Colonel McCombs had encouraged her to stick with, Babe smashed the record in her qualifying round.

"The irrepressible Miss Didrikson showed her mettle in the first heat," Daley wrote. Running over the hurdles in 11.8 seconds and having "caught her teammate, Miss Schaller, with one barrier to clear," Babe crossed the tape in the same time as Simone Schaller. Babe was declared the winner.

Evelyne Hall won the second heat with a time of 12.0 seconds, also besting the previous mark of 12.2 seconds set by South Africa's Marjorie Clark.

The stage was set for the finals. Babe's closest competitors were on either side of her: Hall taking the inside lane, with Babe next, then Clark. Schaller was in lane five.

Babe's teammates watched from the stands. Most were rooting for Hall or Schaller. Anyone but Babe. She may not have had the support of her teammates, but the hushed crowd of eighty-five thousand had come to see Babe. Could she win another gold medal as she'd said in the newspapers? Babe enjoyed making headlines, and she seemed to perform even better with a large crowd cheering her on.

Because starting blocks were banned from the Olympics, Babe and the others used trowels to dig toeholds in the track. Babe jabbed her spikes into the cinders.

A slow starter, Babe was eager to get off faster than she normally did. She focused on the German Olympic official's command to start the race, tense and ready to spring. *"Auf die Plätze!"* the official called. *"Fertig."*

As the gun sounded, Babe was off. She vaulted into the air faster than usual. Then the official's gun sounded a second time and the crowd gasped. Babe had false-started.

Do that again and you're out, Babe knew. Jumping the gun now would mean disqualification and the end of Babe's hopes of winning three gold medals. She had to settle down. Steadying herself into position for a second time, Babe "held back . . . until I saw everybody taking off."

At the halfway mark, "Hall was a yard or perhaps 4 feet ahead of the Babe," noted a reporter. By the fifth hurdle, Babe had caught up with Hall and taken a slight lead, but Hall continued to surge.

After clearing the final hurdle, Hall and Babe sprinted neck and neck to the finish. Babe lunged. Had they crossed the line together? Babe raised her arms in victory, but the finish yarn had caught Hall across her throat, leaving a welt on her neck. It was one of the closest races in Olympic history.

"'Well, I won,'" Hall recalled Babe saying. "I turned and saw some athletes in the crowd cheering me, holding up one finger to show me that I was first," Hall said. "I shook my head and held up two fingers. . . . At that very moment a couple of judges were looking at me."

The judges pored over the photo taken at the finish line by the new "semi-official" Kirby camera. But the hand-timers and the judges had the last say. They seemed hard-pressed to make a decision. Finally, a winner was announced: Babe Didrikson. Hall had finished second—just as she did in the Evanston meet.

Babe won by the width of a fingernail in the closest finish in Olympic history. She was awarded her second gold medal, and she and Hall were both credited with the time of 11.7 seconds: a new world and Olympic record.

HIGHER BRAGGING

Babe was a sensation. Sportswriters focused on her new prediction that she'd win a third gold medal and shatter another world record. No woman had ever won three gold medals in Olympic track and field. Babe would try to do so in the high jump on the final day of competition. Newspapers filled their columns with Babe, calling her "the two-gun girl from Texas," "the one-girl track team," and "the heroine of the meet."

Babe was happy for another reason. Bubba finally arrived and would be in the stands for the high jump. After hearing his plight, the authorities in Oklahoma took up a collection and sent him on his way to California instead of to jail.

Babe took full advantage of the spotlight and raised her bragging to new heights. "Yep, I'm going to win the high jump Sunday and set a world record," she announced. "I don't know who my opponents are and, anyways, it wouldn't make any difference. I hope they are good."

Babe certainly knew who her main opponent was: the jumper who had tied with her in Evanston, Jean Shiley. The afternoon's high jump competition wore on. Babe and Shiley, the only jumpers to clear 5 feet 5 inches—a new world record— were left to battle it out for the gold medal.

"Both of us were better this day than we'd ever been," Babe said.

Shiley had stayed off her feet for three days before the event to save the "spring in her legs." Her teammates pressured her

Babe (arms raised) lunges ahead of Evelyne Hall to win the 80-meter hurdles at the 1932 Games. In one of the closest Olympic races ever, Babe set a world record of 11.7 seconds.

Head or feet? Babe was denied her third Olympic gold medal when the judges determined that she fouled in the high jump. Here she is in midair, clearing the bar in the Western roll style.

to beat Babe, saying, "We couldn't beat her, Jean, *you've* just got to beat her, cut her down to size."

Unlike Babe, Shiley jumped in the traditional, scissor-kick style: crossing over the bar with one foot and landing on the other. She'd tried switching to the Western roll, same as Babe, but Lawson Robertson, her longtime coach, was against it. Robertson was at the Olympics as coach of the U.S men's track-and-field team. He believed the Western roll was too risky, carrying with it the danger of fouling in women's competition. The men's style of jumping was also painful to land. "The pit was sand or sawdust," Shiley said. "You would come down with a big thump and your whole body was jarred. And just think of Babe, she was coming down on her shoulder."

The bar was raised to 5 feet 6¼ inches. Shiley missed, but Babe sailed over the bar with room to spare. "I just soared up there," Babe said. "I felt like a bird. . . . I was up around five-ten, higher than I had ever been, and it was a sensation like looking down from the top of the Empire State building."

When Babe landed in the pit, her foot kicked the bottom of the standard. The bar toppled over. The judges ruled Babe's jump a miss. The gold medal would be decided by a jump-off. Babe shook off her frustration and didn't back down. She was ready to jump again.

With the bar lowered to 5 feet 5¼ inches, both Shiley, then Babe, cleared it handily. Suddenly, the five judges halted the competition to discuss Babe's jump. They decided that Babe's Western roll had been a dive and that her head had crossed over the bar before her feet. Shiley was awarded the gold medal, Babe the silver. The judges made the women coholders of the record.

Babe had made good on her promise to set a new world record. But she was also furious. She'd been jumping the same way all afternoon and was "all twisted" as to why the judges hadn't said anything about her jumping style earlier.

"The collection is spoiled now. That silver medal for the high jump spoiled it," Babe told reporters. "All the rest were golds—firsts." Up in the press box, Grantland Rice told Babe that she had been given "a bad deal."

Shiley agreed with the judges. "All of her jumps over five feet were dives," she explained. "Even our coach—George Vreeland—sent me a note down from the stands and told me that Babe was fouling and that I should turn her in. . . . Babe left the field very, very angry. The other girls on the team were delighted. . . ." "They had a party that evening for me because I had won. [Babe] came to the party late, but she came, and everything was all right."

"Everyone agreed I didn't get a break" in the high jump, Babe said. She decided that "there's no use complaining" and showed admiration for Shiley. "No nicer girl could have won that prize."

Babe had earned three world and Olympic records, two gold medals, and one silver. Her success and popularity elevated women's track and field and helped ensure its place in future Olympics.

PARADE AND ROSES

Some of Babe's teammates traded in their train tickets to buy Olympic souvenirs, taking long bus rides home instead. Babe was on a chartered plane to Dallas, courtesy of Employers Casualty. Ten thousand fans awaited her arrival at Love Field airport. Colonel McCombs was one of them. When Babe saw the Colonel, she threw her arms around him.

Babe rode in the Dallas fire chief's brilliant red automobile during her homecoming parade amid confetti and deafening chants of "Babe! Babe!"

"I was riding in an open car, waving to everybody," Babe said. "I had chill bumps all over that whole day."

Momma, Poppa, and Lillie barely made it to the celebration—they'd driven from Beaumont the night before and had two flat tires. They joined the cheering crowds until Babe spotted them and put out her hand, calling for Lillie to join her.

"Oh, I got *up* there with her, and there were roses all over us, all *over* us," Lillie said. "I cried, we was so happy in all them roses. I didn't know if I should be there, but Babe said it was okay. Because I was with *her*."

Babe's Olympic performance made her a worldwide sensation. "She is beyond all belief until you see her perform," wrote

Babe arrived in Beaumont by chartered plane after her 1932 Olympic victories. Left to right, Mrs. J. M. Gober, Spencer Blain, Hannah Didriksen, Babe, Mrs. Henry Wood of Employers Casualty, Beaumont Kiwanis president W. C. Todd, and Ole Didriksen.

Grantland Rice. "Then you finally understand that you are looking at the most flawless section of muscle harmony, of complete mental and physical co-ordination the world of sport has ever known. . . . There is only one Babe Didrikson and there has never been another in her class—even close to her class."

BABE
VS. THE
UNKNOWN

"People kept telling me how I could get rich if I turned professional. That big-money talk sounds nice when you're just a kid whose family has never had very much."

—Babe Didrikson

"Miss Didrikson is probably the most naïve athlete ever to turn professional. She says what she thinks, let the arrows fall where they may."

—Arthur Daley, *New York Times* columnist

Reporters rushed to interview Babe, eager for the secret behind "the Texas tornado's" athletic greatness. She was the most famous Olympic athlete in the world.

Stories about Babe grew like the seafaring adventures Poppa had told her as a child. Writers stretched the truth. To make Babe's achievements sound more impressive, they wrote that she was a giant "Amazon" or barely five feet tall.

Babe added to her own tales. Already posing as a teenager, she created a different story about her nickname. Rather than explaining that it was Momma's idea, Babe said the name came from her sandlot friends. Since Babe had hit so many home runs growing up, she said her teammates had named her after Babe Ruth.

Hungry for a story, sportswriters questioned Babe about what sport she would conquer next. Babe had no idea. She wanted to be a professional athlete but didn't know how. Babe was determined to play sports and take advantage of her Olympic fame. The next Summer Olympics were four years away.

Grantland Rice was convinced Babe could be a champion in any sport she tried. Other sportswriters didn't believe in Babe like Rice did. To prove his point, Rice urged Babe to test her skills in a golf match. So Babe became part of a bet.

Rice set up a match with three other sportswriters who didn't have much faith in Babe. Westbrook Pegler, Braven Dyer, and Paul Gallico had reported on Babe's heroics at the Olympics. They were certain she would fail at golf. Would Rice's idea build up Babe's legend or would she flop?

Babe liked proving people wrong and took on the challenge. But she hadn't played much golf. Borrowing Bea Lytle's clubs a few times in high school, Babe had played the local course that was infested with snakes. And she'd shot a few rounds in Dallas. That wasn't enough to make Babe certain she could beat the sportswriters.

Babe was nervous, so she showed up at the course extra early and picked up a few pointers from a golf teacher. Rice and Babe challenged Gallico and Dyer to a nine-hole match. They bet a small amount of money on who would win.

At the first tee, Babe held her club like a baseball bat. Putting all her might behind her swing, she whacked the ball hard. The writers were speechless. "She steps up to the ball . . . , bothers not about a practice swing and then slugs the pellet far down the fairway," Dyer wrote. Babe's drive was longer than any of the men's.

Babe works on her golf swing in front of the family home in Beaumont.

Sportswriter Paul Gallico wrote many harsh words about Babe. He was the first to call her a "Muscle Moll."

Approaching the final hole, Babe and Rice led by one stroke. Babe's tee shot traveled 250 yards. Gallico drove his ball farther, but "for a man who outweighs the Babe by 100 pounds, [it] was nothing to brag about," Dyer wrote.

Looking for an edge, Babe dared Gallico to race her to the green. She beat him easily, then joked about how out of shape Gallico was. The run exhausted the writer enough that he failed to win the hole.

"Gallico and I paid off," Dyer said, "perfectly satisfied that the Babe is just as good as she claims."

Gallico wasn't satisfied. He wouldn't forget the humiliation of the defeat. Babe was a champion, but she was a woman. Gallico would seek revenge by writing many harsh, personal attacks about her.

BABE'S NEXT BOAST

Babe never forgot that golf match either. Not only had she impressed the writers with her hefty swing, but she'd become excited about the sport. Conquering it became her new goal. Babe made another bold prediction. She'd compete in the national golf championship in just a couple of months, "and, what's more, I believe I'll win it. I can outdrive most women golfers now."

Babe also needed to earn a living. The golf championship was for amateurs, so there was no money to be won there. Poppa's poor health prevented him from working, and there was still a mortgage on the family's home. Babe returned to Dallas and her job with Employers Casualty.

Babe practiced for the golf tournament and trained for the upcoming basketball season. The rival Illinois Women's Athletic Club offered Babe a $300-a-month job if she'd join their team instead. Babe told the ECC president about the offer. He raised her salary to $300 a month, so she decided to stay in Dallas.

That fall, Babe acquired a red Dodge coupe. Soon after, a newspaper advertisement appeared for that model of car with an endorsement from Babe and a photo of her. The Amateur Athletic Union (AAU) promptly declared Babe a professional. Accepting money for promoting a product was against the rules of amateur sports.

The suspension meant that Babe couldn't compete for the ECC teams or play in amateur golf tournaments. To Babe, it

THE WRITER BEHIND THE "MUSCLE MOLL"

Babe's golf game with four of the leading sportswriters left a negative impression on one of the men she defeated that day in 1932: Paul Gallico of the *New York Daily News*.

After Babe outsprinted him on the fairway during the golf game, Gallico wrote articles attacking Babe's appearance and sexuality. "She was a pathetic and solitary figure," Gallico boldly wrote, "neither one thing nor another in the average, normal world of ordinary men or women or even, for that matter, of athletes."

Gallico's bullying continued until Babe got married several years later. He claimed that the reason Babe had become an athlete was "because she would not or could not compete with women at their own best game—man-snatching."

Gallico labeled Babe a "Muscle Moll." His readers took note, even those close to Babe's home. Gallico's words (and those of a few other sportswriters) made women and girls think twice about pursuing athletics.

"I loved to play softball [as a kid]," said Belle Mead Holm, who served as women's athletic director at Beaumont's Lamar University. "I remember my mother would absolutely *weep* over my going to those games. She used to say, 'Please, I don't want you to grow up like the Babe, Belle. Just don't be like the Babe, that's all I ask.'"

Late in Babe's athletic career, Gallico finally seemed to regret his vicious personal attacks. "I am afraid that we often wrote as though the subjects were blind, or . . . would never see our articles," he admitted. Gallico called Babe brave for bearing "all the jokes that were made about her—mostly having to do with her prowess and masculinity."

This is the automobile that got Babe in trouble with the Amateur Athletic Union after an advertisement for the car appeared with her picture.

seemed like a cheap shot. The suspension "would have been fair enough if I'd given permission for my name to be used in that ad, or taken pay for it," she said. "But I hadn't. A Dodge man in Dallas had set it up on his own. He didn't realize that it would cause any trouble."

The "Dodge man" was E. Gordon Perry, owner of a Dallas car dealership. He told the AAU that Babe let him know how much she liked the car and that he had told Chrysler company

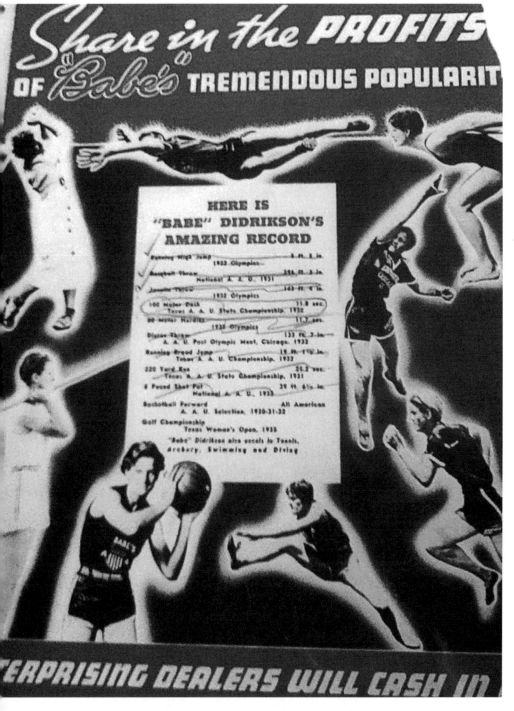

The Chrysler company highlighted Babe's many athletic accomplishments in this advertisement, hoping that her endorsement would help sell cars.

executives about it. Perry said the company had decided to create the ad without Babe's knowledge.

After hearing from Perry, the AAU announced that Babe could remain an amateur. But Babe had already made another decision. She accepted an offer from Chrysler to promote its Dodge brand of cars. Babe said the company was "sorry about what had happened, and they wanted to make it up to me." She would be a professional athlete, even though the money she'd earn from the car company wouldn't be for playing sports.

Babe joked about how strict the AAU's rules were, calling it "a terrifying business" to adhere to the AAU's 350-page rulebook. "I'm afraid I could never memorize all those rules," she said. "I'd rather try to smash another world's record for something."

Avery Brundage, who was the president of the AAU, did not care for Babe's sarcasm. He reminded reporters that "the ancient Greeks kept women out of their athletic games. They wouldn't even let them on the sidelines. I'm not so sure but they were right."

Babe traveled to Detroit to appear at the annual Auto Show. She signed autographs at a booth and played her harmonica to draw people to look at Dodge cars.

Chrysler hired an agent named George P. Emerson to set up money-making events for Babe after the Auto Show. Emerson was an executive with the agency that had produced the Dodge advertisement that got Babe into trouble with the AAU.

He arranged for her to sing and play the harmonica at the Palace Theater in Chicago. Babe would be headlining a vaudeville show, performing up to five times a day.

FIT AS A FIDDLE

Even though Babe was a good musician, she had never sung or danced on a stage. But as with anything else, she was confident that she could do it. On her first day, however, Babe saw a huge crowd waiting to get into the theater. Her name lit up the marquee. "My Lord, I can't go through with this!" she said.

A humorous piano player named George Libbey warmed up the crowd with songs and jokes. Then Babe strode down the aisle wearing a Panama hat, a green swagger coat, and high heels. She belted out a song called "I'm Fit as a Fiddle and Ready for Love."

I'm fit as a fiddle and ready to go
I could jump over the moon up above
I'm fit as a fiddle and ready to go

Babe kicked off her high heels and changed into rubber-soled track shoes. She shed her coat—revealing a red-white-and-blue jacket and silk shorts—and performed a series of athletic stunts. Then she climbed onto a treadmill and started to run.

"They staged it real nice, with a black velvet backdrop and

The Palace Theater in Chicago showcased Babe's singing, dancing, and harmonica playing.

a great big clock to show how fast I was going," she recalled. Babe finished the show with a few songs on the harmonica, including "When Irish Eyes Are Smiling."

A critic for the *Chicago Tribune* was impressed, writing in the next day's paper that "Friday afternoon was the 'Babe's' first time behind footlights, and the girl from the Lone Star State took the hurdle as gallantly as she ever did on the track."

The crowds loved Babe. She received more offers to perform. Babe claimed she'd been promised $2,500 to do a similar show in New York. But this was not how she wanted to earn a living. After a week on the Chicago stage, she quit. Babe was a competitor, not a stage performer. She didn't want to make money just for being famous. She wanted to win championships.

"It was still in my craw that I wanted to be a champion golfer," she said. "I could see I'd never get to do that with these four or five stage shows a day."

Babe traveled to New York for a short time to earn money in some sports exhibitions. She got trounced in a billiards match against world champion Ruth McGinnis. A few nights later, she did better in a game with the Brooklyn Yankees basketball team.

The Yankees' opponent was a team called the Long Island Ducklings. Babe was paid $400 for the game, and she earned it the hard way. She managed 9 points in leading the Yankees to a 19–16 win, but the Ducklings played a bruising style of basketball. "I never got pushed around and fouled so much in any basketball game," Babe said. "If you win through bad sportsmanship, that's no real victory in my book."

By halftime, Babe's pants were split up the side from the rough play. She was offered another pair, but turned them down. She was "all fired up to get back there and show these girls they couldn't stop me with their rough stuff."

After the game, the Ducklings presented Babe with a gift: a live duck. She took it back to her hotel room. "I tried to keep the duck in the bath tub, but it would get out and walk around the room," she said. A couple of nights later, Babe's menagerie grew when she was awarded a little white pig during a contest at a dance. She air-mailed the two animals to her parents.

"Momma and Poppa were nearly going crazy back in Beaumont—ducks coming to the house, and pigs coming," Babe said. Soon she returned home, too.

EYES ON THE GREEN

By the spring of 1933, Babe was more driven than ever to be a champion golfer. She'd saved $1,800 from her stage show and other exhibitions. Babe believed that would be enough to live on for three years in California. "I was going to do nothing but learn golf," she said. She brought her mother and Lillie with her.

In California, Babe met Stan Kertes, a golf teacher. When Kertes saw Babe swing a golf club, he canceled his lessons with other students to focus on her. Babe's powerful drive impressed him, but she gripped the club wrong. It would take time for her

Stan Kertes taught Babe the fine points of the game.

to learn to "read the greens" while putting. Kertes explained that it took most golfers many years to perfect their skills.

Babe found golf harder than any other sport she'd tried—harder than training for the Olympics. For the first time, she'd found a sport that she might not master. She practiced every spare minute, showing up at a driving range as early as 5:00 a.m. after eating Momma's home-cooked breakfast. Babe often stayed at the range until midnight when they turned off the lights.

Kertes had never seen a golfer work so hard. "She hit ball after ball until her hands began to bleed, and I had to make her wear gloves and finally beg her to stop and rest," Kertes said.

Kertes did not charge Babe for lessons, but buckets of golf balls cost 50 cents apiece at the driving range. She also paid the rent for an apartment and bought all the food. Babe had underestimated how much money she needed, and she ran out after a few months. Golf would have to wait.

Babe, Momma, and Lillie returned to Texas. Poppa was quite sick and needed an operation. To help pay for it, Babe went back to work at Employers Casualty, but the family owed a great deal of money for the hospital stay.

Babe was devoted to her loving parents, Hannah and Ole Didriksen.

Poppa recovered but couldn't work. Babe needed to make even more money. A lot of it.

Babe was lost. She considered bowling and tennis, and she even bragged that she might try swimming the English Channel. In 1926, Olympic swimming champion Trudy Ederle had gained worldwide fame by making a record-breaking swim across the twenty-one-mile-wide channel.

Babe dropped those ideas when a new opportunity arrived. Sports promoter Ray Doan offered Babe a chance to tour with a "barnstorming" basketball team. Barnstorming teams traveled from town to town in rural areas, playing against local teams and then moving on. To make the most of her fame, the team was called Babe Didrikson's All Americans.

Most of the players on the team were men, although one or two other women sometimes played. Touring the country, they crammed into a sedan for the long drives to and from the ninety-one games they played in the winter of 1933–34. The team drew big crowds in small towns. Babe was paid $1,000 a month.

In the spring of 1934, Babe pitched an inning or two in a few major league baseball exhibition games. A *New York Times* writer who watched her pitch against the Brooklyn Dodgers reported that she "pitches with a graceful, easy delivery that would do credit to any hurler."

Doan then arranged for Babe to join the House of David men's baseball team, another barnstorming show. She was the

Babe's All Americans barnstormed the country in the winter of 1933–34. Though Babe was often the only woman player, she sometimes was joined by Jackie Mitchell (number 4) and Gladys Crossly (number 8).

only woman this time. All of the men wore heavy beards and they entered the field riding donkeys. Babe was the star attraction and earned more than twice as much as her teammates.

But how could Babe be taken seriously when she was riding a donkey? "Sometimes, . . . I wasn't sure if people were laughing with me or at me," she said.

Babe was a sensation with the donkey-riding House of David baseball team in 1934.

BARNSTORMING BLUES

For Babe, the baseball tour was different than the basketball season in one big way: she did not travel with her teammates. Babe drove by herself to the ballparks. She'd arrive at the game, pitch an inning or two, then leave for the next stop. It was a grueling season, as the team played more than two hundred games. She sent most of her money home and bought a new car for Poppa and a new stove and refrigerator for Momma. She also paid for Lillie's wedding.

Babe drove from town to town alone, ate her meals alone, and stayed by herself in motels. For company, she listened to the radio and played her harmonica. Babe didn't complain, but barnstorming was tiring and lonely.

It wasn't satisfying, either. Babe was earning a living as an athlete, but the baseball games were more like a circus side-show compared with the glory she'd earned at the Olympics. Spectators flocked to see her, so she received plenty of applause and good pay. But Babe was driven by setting records and winning championships. The barnstorming trips offered none of that.

Babe longed for something more suited to her talents. All that travel "was terribly hard on her, physically and emotion-ally," said Ruth Scurlock. "She had to go through with those demeaning travels and those ridiculous games."

The travel did pay off. Babe estimated that she made $40,000 in her first few years after the Olympics, a huge sum in those days. But she'd used most of it to support her family and pay off the mortgage on her parents' house. She didn't have much money at all.

"My name had meant a lot right after the Olympic Games, but it had sort of been going down since then," Babe said. "I hadn't been smart enough to get into anything that would really keep me up there."

Babe knew what the solution was. She had to become the world's best golfer.

BABE
VS.
THE RULES

"Most things come natural to me, and golf was the first that ever gave me much trouble."

—Babe Didrikson

"She had a slight swagger but you don't swagger that way unless you have something to swagger about[,] and she had it."

—Bea Lytle,
Babe's high-school coach

The long basketball and baseball tours were over. Babe needed a job, and Employers Casualty welcomed her back in late 1934. "She was so poor it was pitiful," said one of her friends.

Babe hadn't played much golf in the previous months, but she entered a tournament in nearby Fort Worth anyway. She hoped that a victory would remind the public what a great athlete she was.

Babe's first round was superb—five strokes better than anyone else's. It was like old times. "It did me good to see the headlines in the Texas newspapers the next day," she said. But Babe was rusty from her long time away from golf. She did not play well for the rest of the tournament.

Performing poorly in any sport bothered Babe. The loss in Fort Worth drove her to practice harder than ever and not play another tournament until she was ready.

Babe fixed her sights on the 1935 Texas State Women's Golf Championship. It was a long way off, but she was excited to

Babe had a more powerful golf swing than any woman before her.

have a new title to chase. "No prize I've won, either before or since, looked any bigger to me," she said. "I settled into as tough a siege as I've ever gone through for any sports event in my life."

Just getting better was never enough for Babe. She wanted to be the absolute best. All winter, on Saturdays and Sundays, she played golf for twelve to sixteen hours a day. On workdays she practiced from 5:30 to 8:30 a.m., then hit more shots on her lunch hour. By 3:30 p.m., she'd be back at the golf course.

After a late dinner, "I'd go to bed with the golf rule book." Babe claimed to have read every line of the rule book twenty-five times. She didn't want more troubles like she'd had with the AAU.

"TRUCK DRIVERS' DAUGHTERS"

Not everyone was thrilled when Babe entered the Texas state tournament in April 1935. Peggy Chandler was one of the state's best players, and she thought golf should be just for the "elite." Chandler was a member of the exclusive River Oaks Country Club in Houston, where the matches would be held.

"We really don't need any truck drivers' daughters in our tournament," Chandler said, referring to Babe.

Babe's father wasn't a truck driver, of course, but everyone knew what Chandler meant. She thought working-class

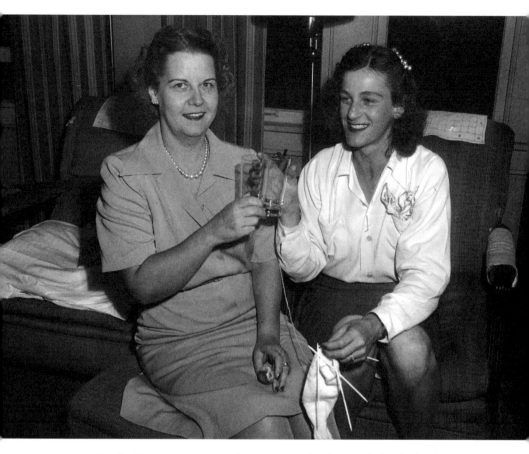

Bertha Bowen was a vocal supporter of Babe's and also helped Babe soften her image.

people didn't belong in golf. Some other players protested that Babe was too masculine to be playing in such a "refined" tournament. They didn't approve of the fact that she had competed against men in other sports.

Bertha Bowen, who was part of the group that organized women's golf tournaments in Texas, disagreed. She knew that those who tried to keep Babe out thought that "it wasn't ladylike to be muscular." Bowen admired Babe. "There's where

[Babe's] courage came in," she said. "I never understood how she had the strength to overlook the snubs and the downright venom of a lot of women."

Babe heard the negative talk. And though she didn't say a word about it, she fought back in her own way. Before the tournament began, she entered a driving contest to see which golfer could hit the ball farthest. Babe made a few silly "girly" swings at the ball to make fun of the "elite" players. Then she blasted a shot the way she usually did, smacking the ball 250 yards to win the contest by a long distance.

The tournament was match play. In that style of competition, two golfers at a time are paired in head-to-head games. Each hole is scored separately. Whoever wins the most holes takes the match. The loser of each match is eliminated from the tournament, and the winner continues to the next round.

Babe won her first three matches, which left her and one other player to determine the title: Peggy Chandler. Chandler had won the tournament before and made it to the championship round four years in a row.

KID VS. VETERAN

The championship match was thirty-six holes—two full rounds. The course was soggy from rain the day before, but Babe played well. She built a large lead. But the more experienced

Chandler came charging back and won the final six holes of the morning round.

It appeared that Babe was caving in to the pressure. "Everybody was saying, 'It's the old story. A kid against a veteran. The kid has folded. She's all through now,'" Babe recalled. But Babe wasn't through at all.

The sun was out by the afternoon and the course was drier. Chandler built a lead, but this time it was Babe who came roaring back to tie.

On the thirty-fourth hole, it looked as if Chandler would break the tie. Her third shot on the par-5 hole landed close to the cup. It seemed certain that she would finish the hole in just four shots. Babe's second shot had landed in a rut behind the green, half covered with water. There didn't seem to be any way she could tie the hole, let alone win it.

"I studied that shot carefully. . . . I thought of everything I'd been taught about how to play this kind of shot," Babe said. Incredibly, the ball rolled into the cup. Just when it looked as if Babe would fall behind, she had taken the lead.

"'Best at Everything' Babe Garners Another Trophy," shouted the headline in *Newsweek* a few days later. Babe had held on to win.

To her credit, Babe didn't mention Chandler's insulting "truck driver" remark. She praised Chandler's golf skills and said she was "a swell girl."

Peggy Chandler wasn't welcoming when Babe entered the 1935 Texas State Women's Golf Championship. She looks friendlier in this photo after Babe won the event.

TROUBLE AGAIN

Babe hoped to win all the big amateur golf tournaments across the country, including the national championship. But within two days of her Texas win, newspapers reported that the U.S. Golf Association (USGA) was looking into her eligibility. "It seemed they'd had complaints from people who thought that because I'd done professional things in athletics, I didn't belong in amateur golf," she said.

The USGA ruled that Babe was not eligible to play golf as an amateur, based on her "activities as a professional in other sports—baseball, basketball and billiards." They said she could play amateur golf in the future, but only if she stopped taking money in other sports for up to three years.

Babe wanted her future to be in golf, so she didn't make any snide remarks as she had when the AAU banned her. But she protested that she'd only been playing golf for a few months and hadn't been paid for any sports lately. "I'd never been a professional in golf."

It was hard to resist taking money, though. Babe went back on the road for more of those gimmicky exhibitions, but this time her only focus was golf. She signed a contract with P. Goldsmith and Sons to promote the company's golf equipment. Fred Corcoran, an agent, set up a tour for Babe with Gene Sarazen, one of the best golfers of the 1930s. They would team up for matches against other top players. Now Babe really was a professional golfer.

The events with Sarazen drew big crowds. Babe was paid

between $250 and $500 for each exhibition, and her deal with Goldsmith was worth another $2,500 a year. "The galleries were huge because they wanted to compare Babe's distances to the men stars," said golf pro Bill Nary.

Babe delighted the crowds on the eighteen-event tour. She'd send a ball soaring down the fairway, then say, "Don't you men wish you could hit a drive like that?"

Sarazen helped Babe improve her game, particularly in hitting shots out of sand bunkers. She often practiced for twelve hours after an event. And she always put on a great show, with trick shots, lots of wisecracks about Sarazen and the other players, and plenty of jokes for the crowd. "I'll break my neck to give the people a good show," she said. "I'll bear down on that old Texas drawl, because they seem to like it, and I'll say . . . today you're looking at the best."

Babe lined up five golf balls, then drove each one. The trick was that the first ball was still in the air after she'd hit the last. She said the tour with Sarazen showed her how to entertain the fans. She kept that up for her entire career, even in the most serious competitions. "I'd kid him, and kid the crowd, and of course he'd kid me some too."

In every city they visited, the tour made newspaper headlines, reminding the fans that Babe was still a great athlete.

But when the tour ended, Babe was faced with the fact that there was only one golf tournament for professional women: the Western Open.

Champion golfer and expert showman Gene Sarazen (in sweater vest) showed Babe how to entertain a crowd.

Bertha Bowen believed that Babe had been treated badly when the USGA didn't let her compete as an amateur. Bowen worked toward adding a second "open" tournament in which amateurs and professionals could all play. Along with her husband, R. L. Bowen, she used her influence to turn the Fort Worth Invitational into the Texas Women's Open.

Babe stayed at the Bowens' home during the new tournament that fall. She didn't win, but her time with Bertha had a big effect. Bertha helped Babe soften her brash behavior. She encouraged Babe to dress in more feminine clothes and to wear makeup, too.

"Some writers have said that around this time a big change took place in me," Babe wrote. "Their idea is that I used to be all tomboy, with none of the usual girls' interests, and then all of a sudden I switched over to being feminine." "But I was always interested in the women's things around the house, like cooking and sewing and decorating. I loved all the pretty things."

Many reporters and other women golfers charged that Babe's "softening" was just part of the show, and that underneath it all she remained crude and masculine.

BACK TO CALIFORNIA

Babe saved a lot of money from the tour with Sarazen. She returned to California with her parents, Lillie, and Bubba. Babe intended to "concentrate on my golf game for a good long while, the way I'd tried to do a couple of years before." She rented a two-bedroom apartment with a fold-down bed in the living room for Bubba.

Babe paid for everything, as usual. Over the next few years, she took more lessons from Stan Kertes, earned a living from clinics and exhibitions, and played in the very few tournaments open to women professionals. But there weren't enough open tournaments to satisfy her need for competition. Then Babe had an idea.

The Los Angeles Open was a men's event, but it was considered "open." Did that mean women could enter, too? Tournament officials didn't think so, but nothing in the rules said that women were banned. So Babe signed up for the 1938 tournament.

The officials decided to make the best of it. They had an idea that might bring more attention to the tournament without causing a distraction for the better players. They paired Babe with another colorful athlete—professional wrestler George Zaharias, who entered the tournament on a whim.

Zaharias had been playing golf with friends and had become quite good at it, although nowhere near the level of the professionals. "One day when he broke eighty and he said as a joke, 'Now I'm ready to enter the Los Angeles Open,'" Babe recalled. His friends goaded him into actually entering.

It was a move that would change George's and Babe's lives forever.

In 1937, Babe Didrikson played with baseball great Babe Ruth in a charity golf match on Long Island, New York. Spectators were in awe of Babe's mighty golf swing.

Babe loved to clown around for the spectators after a golf match was over.

BABE
VS.
THE ROAD

"She wasn't just an athlete, but rather a unique combination of talent, image, personality, and showmanship."

—Melanie Hauser, sportswriter

"He was a great actor, there were no actors like him in wrestling. Famous movie stars used to come to watch him act in the ring."

—Sid Marks, assistant to George Zaharias

George Zaharias was a big, handsome man. Known as the "Crying Greek from Cripple Creek," he'd been a star professional wrestler since 1932. He was flashy and did everything he could to promote himself—a lot like Babe. When he was losing a wrestling match, he'd wail like a big baby. It was all part of the show, and spectators loved it.

When George and Babe approached the first tee at the Los Angeles Open in January 1938, cameras flashed and reporters pushed close. They called for George to put some wrestling holds on Babe, and the two stars obliged.

"He put his arm around me, pretending to apply neck holds and stuff," Babe said. "And I didn't mind it at all."

George didn't mind either. He liked Babe immediately. "When we shook hands, a big thrill went through me," he said. "There was electricity all around us."

Their flirting and joking continued throughout the round.

Outside the wrestling ring, the young George Zaharias was a handsome and fashionable man.

Playing to the crowd was something they both were used to.

The two star athletes attracted a big gallery of spectators. "Those people didn't see too much good golf," Babe said. "My mind didn't seem to be on my game."

Babe's score was a miserable 84, so she knew she wouldn't qualify for the final rounds. But she and George had a second round to play the next day. Babe was looking forward to it. "I already had the feeling that this George Zaharias was my kind of guy, and it turned out that he was thinking I was his kind of girl."

"REAL TEARS"

Professional wrestling is a mix of entertainment and athleticism. Wrestlers take on "good guy" or "bad guy" roles and plan some of the action in advance. George was always a "bad guy" in the ring. "The fans hate me, but pay money to see me wrestle," he said.

George exaggerated his manliness when he was winning a wrestling match. He also exaggerated his grimaces and moans when he was losing—often crying like a toddler. That's how he got his nickname, the "Crying Greek from Cripple Creek." ("Cripple Creek" was the name of a Colorado town near his home.)

"Listen, George Zaharias cried real tears," said assistant Sid Marks, who described himself as George's right-hand man. "Absolutely real tears." George knew what the crowds wanted to see, and he provided it. The sport made him a rich man.

George (left) was the star, but his brothers Tom and Chris and cousin Babe (left to right) were professional wrestlers, too.

Babe and George had refreshments together after their two rounds at the Los Angeles Open, and he invited her to have dinner after round two. They ate steaks with George's two brothers, who were also wrestlers. Babe said she and George watched the third round of the golf tournament together, and then he asked her to go out dancing.

They saw each other whenever they could after that, although both were on the road a lot. Babe was still putting on golf exhibitions and George was wrestling in arenas all over the country.

George started calling Babe "Romance," so she signed her notes to him with that nickname. The courtship continued through the winter and spring. Babe lost in the semifinals of the 1938 Western Open. "But that particular summer, losing a golf match didn't seem to matter as much to me as it ordinarily did."

Babe and George became engaged to be married, but they kept delaying it because of their sports events. Finally, one day in December 1938, when they were both in St. Louis, George said, "We're going to get married this week or call the deal off." Babe agreed, and they married.

George provided support for Babe that she'd never really had. She loved her family dearly, but it was Babe who supported them. George was the first man she could lean on and let down her guard.

"When I first put my arms around Babe in Los Angeles, she was shaking like a leaf," George recalled. "Everyone needs a

*George and Babe were a loving couple. Babe wanted children,
but they did not have any. She had at least one miscarriage.*

foundation. She was being used. She was alone. Her family didn't understand her because she was too famous. She needed somebody she could trust. I gave her that."

George had business experience. He knew Babe had made a lot of money in her career, but she'd never been able to keep much of it. George began managing Babe's finances, her touring schedule, and her endorsements. He pushed her hard but was affectionate. Instead of a honeymoon, he set up a long (and profitable) tour of exhibitions for her in Australia.

The grind of all that touring began to wear on Babe. She'd been on the road for nearly a decade. What she really wanted to do was compete, but there were still only two golf tournaments open to professional women. So in 1940, Babe decided to try to regain her amateur status. If she got it back, she could play in as many tournaments as she wanted.

"Here I'd been practicing all the time, and developed this fine golf game, and about all I could do with it was play exhibition matches," she said. "I wasn't getting a chance to show whether I was the best woman player." Being an amateur would allow her to prove it.

SWEATING IT OUT

The USGA agreed to reinstate Babe as an amateur. But it would be a long three-year wait. And she would not be permitted to earn any money from sports. She "settled down to sweat it out," dropping all of her paid appearances and endorsements.

Unlike before, Babe could now afford to do that. Prior to meeting George, "I had to stay professional, because I needed the money," she said. But her husband "was a top bean in the wrestling business." George was making about $100,000 a year. He had retired as a wrestler in 1939 because of injuries, but he was very successful promoting matches of other wrestlers. Much of the country was still suffering from the aftermath of the Depression, but people found money for entertainment.

Babe won the 1940 Texas Women's Open and the Western Open, but those were the only tournaments she was eligible to play. She was not allowed to collect any of the prize money.

Babe's competitive golf career was mostly on hold. But that didn't stop her. As she'd always done, Babe looked for a new sport to conquer.

Though she'd played very little tennis in her life, Babe picked up a racket. Almost immediately, she began playing sixteen or seventeen sets a day. (Most competitive tennis matches are two or three sets.) "There was hardly a day when I didn't wear holes in my socks," she said.

"In the space of a month she'd become so proficient with a racquet that tennis teachers watched her with pop-eyed amazement," wrote Arthur Daley.

Unfortunately for Babe, it turned out that the rules of amateur tennis were even more restrictive than golf's: once a pro, always a pro. When she learned that she'd never be allowed to play as an amateur, she quit. "The deuce with it," she drawled. She'd find a different sport to play.

George had many business investments outside of wrestling. He was thinking about buying a bowling alley. He and Babe looked at several but never did buy one. "Naturally it wasn't long before I decided to take a whack at this game myself," Babe recalled.

And naturally, she spent incredibly long hours at it. Babe was allowed to compete in amateur bowling competitions, so she took lessons and practiced constantly. She averaged over 170

During a hiatus from golf, Babe became a first-class bowler.

for the King's Jewelry team in the Southern California Major League, leading the team to a league title.

DOING THEIR PART

Babe kept playing golf, too. "I wasn't going to let myself get rusty at my favorite sport." She played at least three rounds a week and also took part in exhibition matches—with all of the money going to charity.

Many of Babe's exhibitions benefited charities for members of the armed services. The United States had officially entered World War II on December 8, 1941. George did his part, too, promoting wrestling matches to raise money for the United Service Organizations. (The USO provides programs and services to soldiers and their families.)

George had been so angry when Japan bombed the U.S. Navy base at Pearl Harbor, Hawaii, on December 7, 1941 that he tried to enlist in the military. He believed that he could teach wrestling moves to soldiers to help them defend themselves. But every branch of the military rejected George because of his wrestling injuries. If George had been allowed to join, Babe planned to enlist in the Women's Army Corps.

Instead, Babe contributed to the war effort with her golf exhibitions. Her partners included movie stars like Bob Hope, Bing Crosby, and Mickey Rooney. The matches attracted a lot of press and kept her in the public eye.

Hope, a comedian, once joked, "There's only one thing wrong about Babe and myself. I hit the ball like a girl and she hits it like a man."

The war had a big effect on athletics, too. Most golf tournaments and other sporting events were canceled, so Babe would not have had a lot of opportunities to play even if she had been an amateur. Even the Olympic Games were canceled in 1940 and 1944.

Babe had a big setback in 1943 when her beloved father died. He had been in poor health for a long time with lung cancer, and he suffered a fatal heart attack. During Ole's funeral, Babe comforted her mother, Hannah. But Momma was the only family member who wasn't crying. This surprised Babe, since her parents had been so close.

"Babe, if I cried, then you children would start fussing over me," Hannah said. She wanted Babe and the others to think about Poppa instead.

Hannah was not in good health either. She suffered from diabetes. Babe stayed close to her and continued to support her financially.

BACK ON COURSE

Babe regained her amateur status on January 21, 1943, and immediately got back to her winning ways. She took first place in a tournament at the Los Angeles Country Club. But many events were still being canceled because of the war. Babe's next big win wasn't until the 1944 Western Open. It was her second victory in that tournament.

No woman had ever won the Western Open three times, so Babe was ready to make headlines in 1945. She traveled to Indianapolis and played well in the early rounds. Then George called with bad news.

Hannah Didriksen had suffered a heart attack. Babe wanted to fly to Los Angeles immediately to be with her mother. "I didn't feel like playing golf any more." But there were restrictions on air and train travel because of the war. Members of the military had first priority for seats.

"Your Momma wants you to finish the tournament," George told her.

Babe phoned her sister Esther Nancy, who was with her mother, but her sister said the same thing. Babe planned to leave anyway. "But with the wartime travel priorities still on, I couldn't get a seat on any plane or train out of Indianapolis."

She won her semifinal match the next day, qualifying for the final. Again she tried to leave. No sporting event was as important to her as her mother. Babe still couldn't get out of town. Momma died that evening.

Babe was heartbroken. She asked competitors Peggy Kirk Bell and Marge Row to have dinner in her room that night because she didn't want to be alone. "Babe just sat there and played her harmonica," Bell recalled. "We didn't really know her

Hannah Didriksen was always proud of her daughter. Babe was brokenhearted when her mother passed away.

and didn't know what to say. She played for hours. She didn't speak, she just played on and on."

Babe won the tournament the next day, saying that she "felt I was playing for Momma."

Her trip home to Los Angeles was as grueling as any tournament. From Indianapolis, she was booked on a 5:00 a.m. flight to Kansas City but was bumped. She waited for several hours before getting on a flight to New Mexico. After another wait, Babe flew to Arizona and then sat for hours in the Phoenix airport. She finally arrived in Los Angeles just in time for the funeral. It was Babe's thirty-fourth birthday.

"I never could cry too easy when I was a kid," Babe said, "but when I saw Momma there that day in 1945, I really broke down. The others just left me alone in the chapel to cry it out."

A RECORD TO REMEMBER

Babe and George soon returned to their busy schedules, but Babe began to yearn for a rest. After winning five straight golf tournaments toward the end of 1946, she was ready for a long break.

George had other ideas. He was always on the lookout for a way to increase Babe's fame. Making headlines meant more fame and more money. George pushed Babe to go to Florida for some winter tournaments to "build that streak up into a record they'll never forget."

Babe resisted. George kept pushing. He said he'd travel

to Florida with her. But as often happened, George discovered some last-minute business obligations that kept him from going.

Babe set out for Florida alone. She won tournaments in Tampa, Miami, and Orlando. Then she called George and said, "I'm tired of traveling around down here by myself." She said she was coming home, but George convinced her to stay on the road and keep playing. "No, honey. Don't do that," he said. "You're in a hot streak. Stay with it."

Her win streak reached twelve before she lost in the first round of the National Open. Babe conveniently forgot that loss. She later claimed that she'd won seventeen in a row.

Babe was definitely ready for some time off. There was no doubt that she'd earned it.

But there was one more tournament on the horizon: the 1947 British Women's Amateur. It was the world's most famous tournament for women, and no American had ever won it. George insisted that a win would put an exclamation point on Babe's winning streak. Many of the top American male golfers had cemented their reputations by winning the British Open or the British Amateur, including Bobby Jones, Walter Hagen, Gene Sarazen, and Sam Snead.

Babe wanted nothing to do with it at first. Then she said she wouldn't go alone. George promised to accompany her if he could rearrange his schedule. Babe had heard that before. She didn't believe George would take time off from his business to travel to Scotland.

Babe stood her ground. She said, "I won't go unless you go with me."

"Sure, honey," George replied. "I'll go with you. I'll make it if I possibly can."

"I know you," Babe said. "You're giving me some more of that old con. You won't go."

Babe was right. She went to the tournament alone.

Champion golfers Sam Snead and Babe were both sponsored by the Wilson Sporting Goods company, so they often did promotional events together.

GOING FOR BROKE

Arnold Palmer, one of the most successful and popular golfers of all time, was still a teenager when he had the opportunity to play eighteen holes of golf with Babe around 1945. She was a superb golfer, of course, but Palmer learned the most from her attitude.

"She talked to me like a buddy and a friend," Palmer recalled in 2009. "But she was also a great performer."

Palmer credited his day with Babe for contributing to his style of play. Throughout his professional career, he used a "go for broke" style that captured a legion of fans known as "Arnie's Army" and nearly one hundred tournament victories. His wins included the U.S. Open, the British Open, the Masters, and the PGA Championship.

Thirty-year-old Arnold Palmer wins the U.S. Open Golf Championship in June 1960.

Babe tees off at the British Women's Amateur Championship in Scotland.

BABE
VS.
TRADITION

"Before Babe it was a game for girls . . . after Babe, it was a business."

—Herb Grassis,
Chicago Daily Sun columnist

"She was very powerful, but it all went rhythmically. . . . It was perhaps not a perfect swing, but it worked for her."

—Gratian Andrew,
Gullane Golf Club member

Babe was often featured in advertisements like this one.

Babe earned a lot of money endorsing products. This photo was used to promote Wilson golf clubs.

The people of Scotland love golf. The sport was invented there, and top players are revered. But they'd never seen a golfer like Babe Didrikson Zaharias. Her impressive record was well known, but few people knew what to expect when she arrived.

The 1947 British Women's Amateur was played at the Gullane Golf Club near Edinburgh, Scotland. "I'd seen many golfers, even at that age," recalled Rena Craigs, who was eleven when she followed Babe around the Gullane course. "She just looked so powerful compared to what I had seen before from ladies." Craigs described the women golfers she knew as "quite straight-laced."

Babe had taken a ship from the United States to England, then a shorter but miserable second boat ride to Scotland. She stood on the crowded deck with her luggage for ten hours in sweltering heat. Soot from the engine blew on Babe and the other passengers.

The villagers of Gullane welcomed her immediately. On her first morning at the North Berwick Inn, Babe said that she'd like to have her favorite breakfast: bacon or ham and eggs. She wasn't expecting to get it. It turned out that the innkeeper had done some planning to make sure Babe's stay was as pleasant as possible. The waiter told her that the manager "went to an American boat and got bacon and ham for your whole stay here."

Babe had arrived in Scotland early, so she practiced for several days. It gave her time to learn the course and to get to know her new fans.

"When I walked back to the hotel in the evening, about ten or fifteen women would come out of houses along those four or five blocks and say 'Would you like tea with us?'" Babe was delighted to accept the invitations. Then she'd hustle back to the inn to meet with reporters and photographers.

The hospitality went further. The Gullane course is on the seaside, with deep, tough grass forming the rough. Sheep wandered the course, grazing on the grass. When a golfer approached, the sheep would step aside into the deeper grass.

But the animals left droppings all over the course.

"When I practiced, they had a fellow in a white coat go along in front of me and clean off the greens where the sheep had been," Babe said.

During a practice round on a wet day, Babe purposely hit her ball into the rough. "Well, I've got to learn how to handle this stuff," she said to herself. As she hit the ball, the stiff grass wrapped around the club, and the handle hit her left thumb, chipping a bone. A doctor treated the injury, and she wore a glove to hide the bandage so no one else would know.

The "thumb stayed sore as a boil," but that may have been a blessing. "I didn't slug the ball quite so hard," Babe said, "and I had better control of it."

Babe expected warm weather, but the June temperature varied greatly during her stay, with mostly cold, damp conditions. She hadn't brought warm clothes, and she was unable to buy any because clothing was still being rationed as a result of World War II. The local newspaper reported on Babe's plight. Villagers sent gifts of heavy clothing to the inn. Among the donations was a pair of corduroy pants that the spectators came to know as her "lucky slocks" (slacks).

REVVING UP THE CROWD

Babe won her opening match, but she didn't pick up the usual energy from the gallery. The Scottish fans were polite and

P. Goldsmith and Sons developed the Babe Didrikson Coordinated
Golf Equipment, which included clubs and golf balls.

S GREAT LINE!

"Babe" Didrikson

GOLF EQUIPMENT—

Your Opportunity for Increased Sales

000 women golfers are using hand-me-down, cast-off clubs.

supportive, but they were nothing like the rowdy American crowds Babe was used to. The Scots would say "well played" or "nice shot," instead of yelling after a good drive or laughing when Babe tried to joke.

Babe wanted to loosen up the spectators and help them have more fun. In her second match, "I began kidding them a little," Babe recalled. "I told them they could make all the noise they wanted to and it wouldn't bother me. I said the noise would make me play better."

Babe won the second match easily, and the fans showed a bit more energy. After the match, she won them over with some trick shots. Babe put a kitchen match on the ground behind her ball on the tee. The match made a loud popping noise "like a small cannon being fired" when she hit it with her club on the way to striking the ball. She smacked a long drive that way, and the ball landed in a sand trap. Babe claimed that she then balanced a second ball on top of the one in the trap, and hit it so the bottom ball flew into the hole while the top one jumped up and landed in her pocket. It sounds virtually impossible.

The crowds grew larger and louder each day, and Babe kept winning. As she had done in the Olympics and on her sports tours, Babe connected best with working-class people like herself. "Probably more so than the upper class," said spectator Rena Craigs.

There was no admission fee for spectators, so everyone could attend. The Scottish people appreciated golf and didn't try to exclude "truck drivers' daughters."

It was more than Babe's power that impressed the fans. She also changed the way they watched the game. "Scottish people are very reserved and quiet," said Craigs, a lifelong member of the Gullane club. But Babe riled up the gallery.

"She just brought the crowd into it," Craigs said. "Not in a horrible way. Some of the men here were very good golfers and they couldn't believe the shots she was making."

The feeling was mutual. Babe enjoyed the crowds as much as they enjoyed her. She trounced Scottish champion Jean Donald in the semifinal. As a sign of good sportsmanship, Babe then coaxed Donald into dancing the traditional Highland fling with her.

"[Babe] was tremendous," said Gratian Andrew, another longtime member of the Gullane club. "Jean Donald was one of our best and she got massacred by her." But the Scottish fans didn't seem to mind. "We appreciate good golf, even if it's an American," she added with a laugh.

Babe advanced to the final against Jacqueline Gordon of England.

The day of the final was warmer, and Babe dressed in a light skirt and sweater. She also put on an old pair of golf shoes because her regular ones had begun to split from all the damp weather. The morning soon turned cold and windy, and Babe was wishing for her warmer clothes. After the morning round ended with Babe and Gordon in a tie, the fans were yelling, "Babe, go git your slocks on."

"SOMETHING ALTOGETHER DIFFERENT"

Babe's visit to Scotland for the 1947 British Women's Amateur Championship left a lasting impression on two young girls who watched her play.

"It was the first time I'd seen a really athletic woman," said Rena (Walker) Craigs, who was eleven when Babe visited Gullane. "She hit the ball like a man."

Craigs recalled Babe's poise and confidence and the trick shots she displayed after a round had ended. But what she spoke most enthusiastically about was Babe's rapport with the fans, particularly kids.

"I was much impressed," she said in 2013. "We just watched her play and then all gathered round and chatted with her, which was certainly not common" with top golfers.

"The village was all golf," she said, so top players visited regularly. "Often golfers don't talk too much to the crowds. She was delightful."

And that Texas drawl? It sounded "very American," Craigs remembered, laughing. "Usually, people are pretty quiet on the golf course. She endeared herself to us."

Mrs. Craigs is still a member of the Gullane Golf Club, and she still has the autograph book Babe had signed sixty-six years earlier. The excitement of watching Babe play had helped her develop a lifelong devotion to the game. "She certainly made me keener on golf," she said. "You don't meet many people like that in life."

Gratian (Salvesen) Andrew was sixteen that year, but she was away at school in St. Andrews when Babe was at Gullane. Fortunately for the teenager, Babe included St. Andrews in her post-tournament tour of Scotland.

"My father was very keen on golf and sport," she recalled in 2013. "He rang me up and told me he was coming to St. Andrews to see her play. He told the house mother I was going with him."

As Babe played, they walked the famous Old Course with her, along with a modest-sized crowd that grew as the day progressed. Mrs. Andrew's most lasting memory is of Babe's tee shot at the seventeenth hole. That hole is one of the most famous—and most difficult—in all of golf. It's known as the Road Hole because a road runs alongside it for most of its length. The tee shot is a blind one: golfers can't see the green. These days, a hotel blocks that view. But in

Babe's day, a series of rail sheds did the same. The sheds made it nearly impossible to hit a straight shot to the green.

"Babe drove clear over the sheds instead of going the normal way," Mrs. Andrew said. "It had certainly not been done by a woman before. I don't know how many men had done it; probably a few big hitters. It was a straight shot to the hole, but a dangerous one. I always think of Babe when I watch someone play that hole."

Mrs. Andrew said that seeing Babe play had influenced her own approach to the game. "For a while I was one of the longer hitters in Gullane club," she said. "But length isn't everything." She noted that Babe was also a great chipper and putter. "But at sixteen, it was the length that impressed me.

"She was very powerful, but it all went rhythmically. She was obviously an athlete from the way she moved. It was perhaps not a perfect swing, but it worked for her."

Mrs. Craigs and Mrs. Andrew were touched by Babe's warm personality and genuine affection for her fans. "She was such a gregarious person; she won people over," Mrs. Andrew said. "She was something altogether different."

Babe's victory at the 1947 British Women's Amateur transformed women's golf. Spectators had not seen such a powerful swing—by a woman—and such a chatty golfer. She had a big effect on young Rena (Walker) Craigs, who is pictured to Babe's left, waiting for an autograph.

Babe switched to her "lucky slocks" during the lunch break. "But I didn't do it for luck," she said. "I was just cold!" She also visited a shoemaker's shop to see if she could get her split shoes repaired but found the shop closed. A handwritten sign in the window read: *Sorry. Closed. Gone To See The Babe.*

Someone tracked the shoemaker down at the course. She was thrilled to do whatever she could for Babe. She fixed the shoes in time for the afternoon round.

Babe pulled way ahead in the afternoon and won easily, celebrating the victory by hurdling a brick wall and dancing more Highland flings. During the presentation of her trophy, she showed how much she appreciated her new fans. Babe sang "a little Highland song I'd learned from some of the Scottish golf pros in the United States—hoping I'd have this occasion to use it. And everybody seemed to like that touch."

She also pulled the bandage off her thumb, revealing the injury for the first time.

Babe stayed in Scotland for a few days to play some of the country's famous courses, including the Old Course at St. Andrews, where golf had begun around seven hundred years before.

BACK TO THE PROS

Babe's trip home was aboard the RMS *Queen Elizabeth*. George arranged for a tugboat filled with reporters and photographers to meet the ship as it approached New York City.

Babe made a big splash when they arrived. She and George donned kilts and danced a Highland fling. Then Babe gave two hours of interviews on board the ship.

Babe wanted to take full advantage of her fame. She and George stayed in New York and began fielding offers for appearances and endorsements. "It got to the point where I stood to make a fast half-million dollars if I'd turn professional again," Babe said.

Fred Corcoran, who was now the promotional director of the men's Professional Golfers Association tour, offered to represent Babe if she'd turn pro. Corcoran was the agent for baseball stars Ted Williams and Stan Musial, and he had helped arrange Babe's tour with Gene Sarazen back in 1935.

Babe and George also met with sportswriter Grantland Rice, who had been an admirer of Babe's since her Olympic days. After the interview, he wrote, "I spent a short half hour at their hotel quietly celebrating with Babe and George Zaharias— two wonderful kids, who I feel constitute an unusually warm and wonderful American love story."

Whether that was still true was anybody's guess. Babe was annoyed that George didn't travel with her. His constant pushing for her to be on the road left little time for romance.

Corcoran took over from George as Babe's promoter and manager, lining up exhibitions and contracts. Babe claimed that Fred consulted with George on everything, but she seemed to rely on her husband less and less. She soon announced

George watches Babe warm up for a golf match. After he retired from wrestling, he lost his muscular physique.

that she was turning pro again.

Corcoran knew that Babe was a grand showman. He wanted to start a professional golf tour for women, and Babe would be the key to making it work. "She had a flair for the dramatic and a raw, earthy sense of humor," Corcoran said. With Babe as the star, he believed the tour would attract lots of interest.

In the meantime, Babe did whatever it took to stay in the public view. She hit golf balls off the diamond at major league baseball games. Corcoran got her a lifetime contract with Wilson Sporting Goods to market Babe Zaharias golf equipment, and deals with Serbin clothing, Timex watches, and other companies.

THE LADIES' TOUR

Babe began entering golf tournaments again as a professional, but there were still very few. "That was the one fly in the ointment for me," she said. So she, George, and Corcoran began planning the golf tour, which would feature a string of new tournaments. The Weathervane sports clothing company agreed to sponsor the first events, and the tour began in May 1949 as the Ladies' Professional Golf Players Association (LPGPA—it was soon shortened to LPGA).

Babe won the first tournament by thirteen strokes, pocketing the first prize of $1,000.

To make sure the tour succeeded, Babe did much more than

play golf. She worked tirelessly, phoning sponsors and persuading them to offer prize money. She also convinced other golfers to turn pro. She was constantly on the phone on behalf of the tour.

George and Corcoran battled about promotion and other concerns. George's involvement annoyed many of the players. He was bossy and disrespectful. "Women's golf belongs to me," he once said. "It's a racket, golf is, just like wrasslin' and the boxin' racket." Babe and George grew farther apart emotionally as she prospered on the tour.

Babe now had the full limelight, overshadowing the other players and winning more often than she lost. She was dazzling the fans with clinics before the tournaments, earning an extra $1,000 each time. Other women were lucky to get $25 for a clinic. The other players resented this, especially when Babe said things like "*I'm* the star and all of you are in the chorus."

But it was true. None of the other players could attract spectators and sponsors like Babe could. There would have been no LPGA without her, and Babe knew it.

"She made it very, very hard on a lot of these women golfers because she'd walk right up and say, 'What are you girls practicing for? You can't win this tournament,'" said Betty Dodd, who joined the tour in 1950. Dodd also said Babe was not a good sport about losing, even at cards or table tennis.

Babe had hardened. She'd put in so much work in her career that she felt she deserved to get all the money and fame she could.

Promoters provided Babe with free hotel rooms, and

BEST OF THE CENTURY

The Associated Press (AP) named Babe Didrikson Zaharias the Woman Athlete of the Year three times in a row: 1945, 1946, and 1947. She'd also earned the award after her Olympic successes back in 1932.

"During all those years in between, what with my troubles over professionalism and everything, I hadn't been able to compete enough to establish whether I was the No. 1 woman athlete," she said.

Babe won the award again in 1950 and 1954. In 1950, the AP also named her the Woman Athlete of the Half Century. In 1999, she was selected by the AP, ESPN, and other organizations as the best of the entire century.

sometimes they paid her extra money just to have her in their tournaments. Dodd said Babe "was never charged anything and if you were with her you wouldn't be charged either. I never had so many free meals in my life."

Babe also tried to appear more feminine, as Bertha Bowen had taught her. But competitor Betty Hicks said, "Babe remained back-alley tough and barroom crude." Still, Hicks and the other women knew the tour would never succeed without Babe.

"Oh, how she gave them a show!" Hicks said. "None of the others of us could have, would have dared." Hicks said that while a player might describe a poor round to reporters by saying "[I] couldn't have hit a washtub with my putts," Babe would pull no punches and say she "couldn't hit an elephant's . . . with a bull fiddle."

BABE'S MENTAL EDGE

One golfer who was outspoken in her dislike for Babe was Louise Suggs. Suggs was the second-best player on the tour, but she received almost no attention compared to Babe.

Suggs often accused Babe of cheating, but other golfers saw Babe's actions as simple intimidation. "Would she try to get a mental edge over us? Sure, all the time. But that's not cheating," said fellow competitor Marilynn Smith.

That "mental edge" sometimes came in infuriating ways. One time, when Suggs was lining up an important putt, Babe gave a blast on her harmonica. Suggs missed the putt, and she never forgave Babe for that one.

In 1951, Babe won seven of the tour's twelve tournaments. Her take was about $15,000, but she made far more from exhibitions and other public appearances. At the end of that lengthy season, she went to her new house on a golf course in Tampa, Florida, which she and George had purchased. It was a small building that had once been a "caddy house." Babe was ready to relax and "spent considerable time making chintz curtains."

Some people say that Babe was thinking about divorcing George. She was less tolerant of his demands and was bothered that he now weighed more than four hundred pounds. He had sloppy eating habits—dribbling food on his shirt—and would eat a stick of butter as if it were a banana. He was also drinking a lot of alcohol.

"After a while [he] got to be a burden to her," Betty Dodd said. "He wanted to push her as hard as he could. To the next tournament, the next exhibition, the next this, the next that."

Betty was a freckle-faced redhead and quite a bit younger than Babe. She was nineteen when she joined the tour, and Babe was thirty-nine. Betty idolized Babe, and they became close companions. They traveled to tournaments together, and Betty began living at the Tampa house with Babe and George. "We always

Babe and her friend Betty Dodd often played music together when they weren't playing golf. Some people speculated that they had a romantic relationship.

Babe was a talented harmonica player and recorded this solo record.

had a lot more fun when he wasn't around," Betty said.

George would leave for weeks at a time. He explained to Babe that he was checking on his business investments. When they were together, she and George often argued. "We started getting at each other's throats much of the time," George admitted.

George also didn't care for Betty, and it annoyed him that Babe spent so much time with her.

Babe had found others to rely on. Though many of the players resented Babe's success, she became good friends with a few of them. She and Peggy Kirk Bell often roomed together while touring. Betty Hicks said Babe was a constant source of practical jokes. Babe's circle of friends had always been small, but she valued those she got close to.

LOSING HER ZIP

Babe began to tire during the 1952 season. She'd had pain and swelling on and off on her left side for several years, but she'd never seen a doctor about it. A hot bath usually gave her relief. The pain grew steadily worse that year, and she finally flew alone to Beaumont to see her family doctor, W. E. Tatum.

Dr. Tatum discovered that Babe had a strangulated femoral hernia, which was stopping the flow of blood at the top of her thigh. It was a serious condition, requiring surgery.

"Doctor Tatum told me that if I'd let it go another week

I might have been a goner," Babe said. She went home to Tampa to recuperate after the operation. Later in the year, she won the Texas Women's Open, but she was physically exhausted.

Babe played poorly in the early part of the 1953 season. On her return to Beaumont for the first Babe Zaharias Open, she made an appointment to see Dr. Tatum again. She was worried because she hadn't recovered any of her usual energy. She'd also noticed blood in her stool recently, so she had an idea of what might be wrong.

Babe lines up a putt during the 1953 Babe Zaharias Open at the Beaumont Country Club.

Babe played well in the tournament, but she was losing steam in the final round. She needed to make a birdie on the final hole to win. That seemed unlikely when she hooked her drive and it landed behind a tree. Babe wasn't shaken. She pulled off a great second shot that left her ball six feet from the hole. "Then I knocked in my putt for the birdie I needed to win."

The hometown fans went wild, and television cameras caught the celebration. But Babe felt awful. "As soon as I could get away I went right up to my room and stretched out on the bed," she said. "I'd never felt so completely played out."

The next day, Dr. Tatum checked the area where he'd performed the hernia surgery. "Then he probed around some more," Babe recalled. "I could see his face out of the corner of my eye. All of a sudden he just turned white.

"He didn't say a word. I guess I'd suspected all along what my trouble was. I said to him, 'I've got cancer, haven't I?'"

Babe in 1954 with her golf-club pin.

BABE
VS.
CANCER

"I don't know yet if surgery will cure her, but I will say that she never again will play golf of championship caliber."

—Dr. W. C. Tatum

"I was determined to come back and win golf championships just the same as before."

—Babe Didrikson Zaharias

It had been three days since Babe's family doctor had sent her to Fort Worth for medical tests. She and George held hands as they waited nervously for the results. A specialist, Dr. W. C. Tatum (who was no relation to Dr. W. E. Tatum), told them what Babe feared. She had cancer.

The tests had shown that Babe had a malignant tumor in her rectum. Instead of traveling to Arizona for the Phoenix Women's Open golf tournament, Babe would be having cancer surgery right away.

The news struck Babe "like a thunderbolt." Poppa had died of cancer. Babe struggled to hear what the doctor explained beyond the words "cancer" and "surgery."

"I thought I was prepared for it," Babe said. "I was crying when we went down on the elevator. George was all distressed. He had never seen me cry before." Babe worried how George would cope.

Dr. Tatum told Babe that her golf career was over. In a burst of frustration, Babe offered her golf clubs to her friend

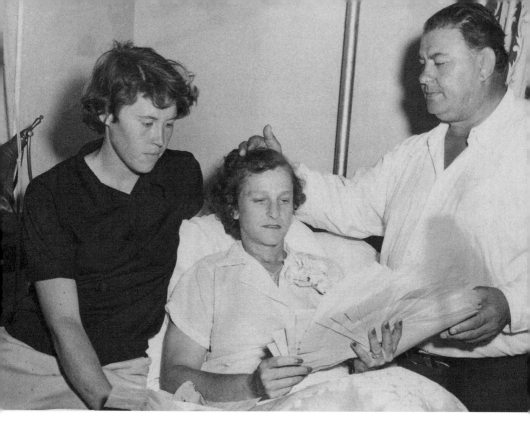

*While in the hospital, Babe (shown with Betty and George)
received thousands of letters from supporters and from others
who were suffering with cancer. She served as an inspiration to
many cancer patients.*

R. L. Bowen, Bertha's husband. "I won't be needing them any
more," she said. But she didn't feel sorry for herself for long.

Betty Dodd was visiting her parents in her hometown of San
Antonio, Texas. She'd expected to drive to Phoenix with Babe and
George. When she heard the bad news, Betty drove to Beaumont
instead. Betty had been a nurse's aide in high school, so she set
up a cot for herself in Babe's room at Beaumont's Hotel Dieu
Hospital. She would help take care of Babe after her surgery.

Doctors declared to the media that Babe would never play
championship golf again. *Time* magazine wrote about the end

of Babe's "fabulous career in big-time sports." Reading the headlines, Babe refused to believe it. The golf clubs Babe had offered to R. L. Bowen were carried into her hospital room. They'd remind Babe of what she intended to do.

A DEADLY OPPONENT

Babe decided to approach cancer as a foe she had to conquer, like in championship golf. No one, including celebrities or athletes, had taken a public attitude toward cancer before. Baseball star Babe Ruth had kept news of his throat cancer a secret. It wasn't until his death in 1948 that the public learned the truth. Columnists wrote how they admired Ruth for dealing with the disease quietly.

Babe Didrikson Zaharias was not quiet about her cancer. As she had in the Olympics and in golf, Babe made bold proclamations about her recovery. She also predicted her own comeback. "I made up my mind that I was going to lick it all the way," Babe said. "I not only wasn't going to let it kill me, I wasn't even going to let it put me on the shelf. I was determined to come back and win golf championships just the same as before."

In 1953, living an active life after having cancer wasn't imagined. People were too terrified of the disease to discuss it. Even the word "cancer" was rarely mentioned. Writers called cancer a "malady" or "malignancy." At first, the media reported Babe's prognosis the same way, avoiding the word "cancer."

Babe spoke openly about her cancer. She made the public aware of the disease. Phrases like "cancer fight" and "cancer consciousness" became more common. Babe gave cancer patients a voice. "I believe the cancer problem should be out in the open," she announced. "The more the public knows about it the better."

Babe's approach to cancer was as radical as the surgery she needed to remove it. The colostomy operation would change Babe's anatomy. Her intestinal tract would be rerouted to dispose waste through an opening in her abdomen and into a colostomy bag wrapped around her waist. Babe had difficulty pronouncing the name of the surgery. She also didn't like the idea of her body being "changed permanently like that." Secretly, Babe hoped the colostomy wouldn't be necessary and that all of the cancer could be removed.

George requested that the hospital recruit the top surgeon for Babe. "I don't care what it costs," he said. Dr. Robert Moore from John Sealy Hospital in Galveston would perform the operation.

Thousands of letters poured in for Babe from cancer patients and well-wishers. Some simply said "To Babe" on the envelope or had newspaper photographs of her taped to the front.

"First they were bringing me letters by the handful," Babe explained. "Finally, they had to use a big wicker clothes hamper. . . . I must have received about 20,000 letters. . . . It really bucked me up to know that I had so many folks all over the world pulling for me."

Celebrities like Bob Hope and Grantland Rice wired or telephoned to wish Babe good luck.

On April 17, twelve days after winning the golf tournament named in her honor, Babe was ready for surgery. She asked to see her old friend and sportswriter Tiny Scurlock. "I'm tired of being on the sports page," Babe told him. "Put me on page one."

Babe made it to the front page.

George chats with Beaumont Journal *sports editor Tiny Scurlock in this 1953 photo. Scurlock corresponded with Babe throughout her life.*

When Babe was wheeled out of the operating room after the four-hour surgery, she asked George, a "colostomy, honey?"

"Yes. It's all right," George said.

But George and Betty had received more shocking news. During the operation, Dr. Moore discovered that Babe's cancer had spread to her lymph nodes. The cancer would likely affect Babe again within a year. Dr. Moore urged George and Betty to keep the news a secret. Not letting the patient know the worst news was a decision many doctors favored in 1953. Betty and George agreed not to tell Babe that her cancer had spread.

LONG ROAD BACK

It took Babe forty-two days to recover in the hospital. "I didn't know exactly where I was or what I was saying," Babe said about the first few weeks. "I'd start to jerk my arms, and the needles that were stuck in there for the intravenous feeding would come out. But Betty found she could stop that by grabbing my hand and telling me not to pull."

Babe was also cared for by Sister Moynihan and the other Roman Catholic nuns who ran the hospital. Soon, Babe reflected on her own faith. "I have never been what you'd call a real church-going Christian," Babe admitted. "But when you get sick, God is the one you go to. He gives you the spiritual muscle that you need."

Babe is all smiles as she leaves the hospital after her first bout with cancer. She's joined by her sister-in-law Mrs. Louis Didriksen (left) and sister Lillie.

234

Babe "did have faith in divine power aiding you when you were in a jam," Ruth Scurlock said, "and that went for her illness, too."

Though thin and weak, Babe visited the children's ward, hoping to cheer the kids up in the same way those letters lifted Babe's spirits. Babe also met Sister Tarsisis, a nun who was a patient across the hall. Sister Tarsisis was afraid to have a colostomy. Babe convinced her to have the operation.

Babe kept eyeing her golf clubs in the corner of her room. She began exercising in her hospital bed. "I started raising one leg up in the air, and then the other. I was working my muscles and pushing them—working my arms and my legs."

By June, Babe was back home in Tampa. She started practicing golf. "A colostomy is a big change," Babe said, "but the body can adjust to it." Soon, Babe felt ready to prove it to the world. She set her sights on a tournament. "Let's go play the Tam," she told Betty, referring to the Tam O'Shanter Open.

Babe called the tournament director in Illinois with a request. The director was concerned that Babe might ask him to break tournament rules by letting her ride in a cart. Professional golfers had to walk the course.

"I don't want a cart," Babe assured him. "I just want to have Betty Dodd paired with me every day." Babe wasn't certain how well her body had adjusted. Having Betty nearby would help if the colostomy bag gave her any trouble.

POWER OR PERIL?

In July, fourteen weeks after her cancer surgery, Babe walked up to the tee at the Tam O'Shanter tournament. A crowd of five thousand spectators gathered. Some hovered just a few feet away, eager to watch Babe play. "Guess I gotta go," she whispered.

Babe felt timid. A colostomy bag was hidden under her clothes. She was afraid of what might happen when she unleashed her powerful swing. "You go out there thinking you're going to hit it hard and then you feel like you're going to pull everything loose and you ease up on it," Babe said.

The colostomy bag held, but Babe's golf game was not what she'd hoped for. "It seemed like I couldn't do anything right," Babe recalled. "I was beginning to think it was true what so many people had said, that I'd never be able to play championship golf again."

Babe was tired and slow on the greens. George held a "sit-stick" for Babe to rest on between shots. By the third day, Babe's game hadn't improved. Disgusted with her score, Babe broke down and cried.

"Babe, quit," Betty advised. "They'll all understand."

"I'm not a quitter," Babe insisted. She finished the tournament in fifteenth place. It was an incredible accomplishment, but not good enough for Babe. "To me, shooting tournament golf doesn't just mean getting a respectable score and finishing up

Babe holds a basket of carnations after winning the first Babe Zaharias Open in 1953, twelve days before she had surgery.

among the leaders," Babe said. "It means being able to win."

The next week, Babe leaped closer to her goal, finishing third in the World Golf Championships, right behind her main rival, Louise Suggs. Babe was back.

Reporters wrote of Babe's courageous return and her gritty fight to play competitive golf. She earned the first Ben Hogan Award, named after the famous golfer who had survived a devastating car crash and returned to be a champion. Babe received more votes for the award than baseball player Ted Williams. Williams had fought with the U.S. Marines in the Korean War and was playing with the Boston Red Sox again.

Babe told reporters she was lucky. She felt that she had beaten cancer, thanks to an early detection. Babe reminded others not to delay a doctor's visit. She vowed to continue fighting cancer "with all I've got." Babe had no idea Dr. Moore had found cancer cells in her lymph nodes. All Babe knew was that she needed a win.

BABE'S BIGGEST THRILL

The following year—1954—Babe was hungry to clinch a golf victory. It had been ten months since her operation. But the closest Babe had come was second in the St. Petersburg Open. Her confidence sank. The press doubted she could win, too. "People were beginning to ask each other whether I'd ever be capable of winning tournaments again," Babe remembered.

"And I was asking myself the same thing."

Babe dug deeper and aimed for the Serbin Open in Florida. She'd received crates of fan mail compelling her to fight on. "Those letters sort of built up my determination to continue in golf," Babe said.

With thousands of fans rooting for her, Babe's desire to win took on a new meaning. She believed winning would not only keep her going but also inspire thousands of others battling cancer and other problems in their lives.

Babe tested her new confidence at the Serbin Open. On the last day, she was tied for first with Patty Berg. Babe grew tired on the back nine but wouldn't give in.

The last hole would determine the winner. Babe's shot landed in a cluster of palm trees. Somehow, Babe would have to slice her ball through the trees. Babe swung hard. Her ball smashed through a palm frond and onto the fairway. Then she reached the green. Babe could taste victory. She sank her putt. Babe had fought cancer and won another championship.

"I guess I'll have to call this the biggest thrill of my life," Babe said. "I didn't think I would ever win another one."

President Dwight Eisenhower invited Babe to the White House. He chose Babe to help kick off the annual Cancer Crusade, and he also wanted to congratulate her on what she'd achieved. President Eisenhower, an avid golfer, held the Sword of Hope, the symbol of the American Cancer Society, like a golf club. Babe gave him tips on his swing.

Babe's focus on life changed because of cancer. When Babe's close friend Peggy Kirk Bell gave birth to her first child, Babe rushed to take a plane to North Carolina. Friends were cherished, and Babe now made time for them. Excited that Peggy's child was a girl, she tried to coax Peggy into naming her little daughter "Babe."

Peggy named the baby Bonnie. Babe didn't mind. She offered some advice to the new mother. "All boys are good athletes," Babe said. "But there aren't many girls who are. Girls can become great athletes easily."

Babe's comeback had been anything but easy. In July 1954, she entered the U.S. Women's Open in Peabody, Massachusetts. It was her first major tournament since the surgery.

Babe took a commanding lead. She tore through the course with a blazing score of 72 on the first day. She fought through her bouts of afternoon exhaustion and shot a second round of 71. Babe was playing the best golf of her life.

On the final day, the gallery cheered and roared for Babe. By the end of the round, she had won her third U.S. Open, finishing an amazing twelve strokes ahead of her closest competitor, Betty Hicks.

Babe bowed to the cheering crowd and appeared humbled. Babe was no longer just winning for herself; she was winning for cancer patients, too.

Babe's victory was declared "the most incredible athletic feat of all time, given her condition." She'd become more than just a sports hero. "I'm happy because I can tell people not to be afraid of cancer," Babe told reporters. "They need not be afraid of an operation."

Babe had proved she could come back and live her normal life of championship golf. "That was her greatest accomplishment," said Ruth Scurlock. Babe "had conquered not only physical weakness but she had conquered [a] pretty good mental hazard. . . . Not her mental hazard, I guess it was the other people's. She was always sure that she could come back."

The Associated Press voted Babe Female Athlete of the Year for the sixth time. No athlete—male or female—had been selected so many times.

After her U.S. Open win, Babe telephoned her doctors. She thanked them for what they had done and insisted that her victory was their victory, too.

"You did it yourself, Babe," Dr. Moore replied.

Babe's courage, determination, and willpower astounded both doctors. Had Babe really "licked" cancer? The few people who knew the secret of Babe's cancerous lymph nodes would have to wait and see.

Babe seemed unstoppable. But in 1955, she felt fatigued again, even away from the golf course. Exhausted and unable to finish the Sarasota Open in February, Babe went for a checkup. She was diagnosed as anemic and told to rest for a while.

Babe and George had talked for years about building their dream home near the Tampa Country Club. They decided that the time had arrived. Babe walked with George and her poodle, Bebe, on the land where they hoped to build. Babe spotted a rainbow and decided to call their home Rainbow Manor.

While Rainbow Manor was being built, Babe vacationed on the Gulf Coast with Betty Dodd and Dodd's sister. Betty's car got stuck in some mud, and Babe helped push it out. A searing pain shot through Babe's back.

Despite the pain, Babe traveled to South Carolina that April, intent on playing in the Peach Blossom tournament. Babe was eager to keep the LPGA successful. She knew that tournaments drew bigger crowds "when all of us are in there than when some of us aren't." This was a new Babe, willing to help other players succeed. Babe won the Peach Blossom by four strokes. It would be her last tournament.

Babe's back pain continued and became severe. Doctors at John Sealy Hospital in Galveston thought the cause was a herniated disc. But after they operated on Babe's spine, she felt just as much pain. Yet she still planned her next tournament. "You've proved everything. You don't have to prove anything more," George told her.

"At times I feel I'd rather just ride around the course in my electric cart . . . and let the rest of the girls fight it out," Babe admitted. "It used to just kill me to get beat. I guess I've mellowed down."

Sensing that Babe's health condition was serious, Fred Corcoran asked her to write her life's story. She dictated it to sportswriter Harry Paxton.

In July, just as the book was finished, doctors found the cause of Babe's pain. The cancer had spread to her sacrum near the pelvis. There was no way to operate. Babe would have to write another chapter in her autobiography. Prepared to fight cancer a second time, Babe refused to accept that she would never play golf again.

"There are several reasons why I didn't retire from golf after that 1953 cancer business—and still don't intend to retire," Babe wrote. "With the love and support of the many friends I have made, how could I miss? . . . Maybe I'll have to limit myself to just a few of the most important tournaments each year. But I expect to be shooting for championships for a good many years to come. My autobiography isn't finished yet."

Babe never regained her strength. By Christmastime, George wrote a letter to the Bowens on Babe's behalf, saying that they probably wouldn't be able to make their annual trip to Fort Worth. Babe and George's seventeenth wedding anniversary was December 23 and they liked to celebrate it with Bertha and R. L.

The Bowens decided to bring George and Babe to Fort Worth anyway. After picking them up in their private plane, they drove Babe to a golf course and helped her out of the car.

"I just wanted to see a golf course one more time," Babe said.

In January 1956, George drove Babe to Sarasota, Florida. They watched Betty Dodd play in a tournament. She lost by one stroke. "I was dying to win it because Babe was there, but I just didn't," Betty said with regret.

By June, Babe's condition had deteriorated. She asked to be taken to John Sealy Hospital. This time, Lillie moved in to take care of Babe. Lillie slept on a cot next to her sister, who "held my hand all the time, but she was always thinkin' of others, that girl was."

Babe made it to her forty-fifth birthday that June. She died on September 27, 1956.

President Eisenhower honored Babe's memory by calling for a national moment of silence. Newspapers around the world paid tribute to Babe, recounting her many accomplishments. Babe had become the greatest woman athlete in the world, conquering every sport she'd attempted. Yet she had succeeded beyond winning. Babe broke barriers and changed attitudes about what women could achieve. Her unfailing spirit and determination through any obstacle had made her a hero.

"I know she'll live forever in the hearts of millions," George said.

The *New York Times* printed Babe's legacy on the front page: "She didn't know the meaning of the word quit, and she refused to define it, right to the end."

But perhaps the best compliment about Babe was given by Rev. C. A. Woyteck at her funeral service. "She was always just Babe," he told her friends and family. "She never lost the common touch."

Babe adored her poodle, Bebe.

POST-MATCH

Every great woman athlete who triumphs in her sport or changes it has Babe Didrikson Zaharias to thank. Four-time Olympian Jackie Joyner-Kersee credits Babe as her inspiration for pursuing track and field. Joyner-Kersee won two Olympic gold medals in the seven-event heptathlon, but Babe had been track and field's first female multisport star more than half a century earlier. And while professional women golfers can now earn $1 million or more in a single season, they might not have had that opportunity if Babe hadn't paved the way by almost single-handedly making the LPGA a success.

Babe did incredible things in sports. World records and Olympic gold medals. Championship basketball seasons. Spectacular victories in golf. It's hard to imagine a greater athletic achievement than Babe's third U.S. Women's Open golf victory in 1954—a year after doctors told her she'd never play again.

Yet if you ask a classroom of students who "the Babe" was, they'll respond by talking about baseball hero Babe Ruth. Why do children want to grow up to be like Babe Ruth and know very little about Babe Didrikson Zaharias?

As journalists, we longed to find out. We also felt a responsibility to keep Babe's story alive. We traveled to her hometown of Beaumont, Texas, and read all the letters she'd sent to Tiny Scurlock. We listened to interviews with her friends and family

Babe Ruth was known for baseball, but he played golf with Babe Didrikson several times. Babe liked to say she'd been named for the famous baseball star, but the nickname had come from her mother.

This life-size painting of Babe is on display at the Babe Didrikson Zaharias Museum in Beaumont, Texas. It's signed "Luis A. Vazquez, '51."

members. We walked the streets where she had grown up and imagined her hurdling those hedges on Doucette Avenue.

Was Babe's legacy largely unnoticed a half century after her death because the sports she had conquered weren't as popular as Babe Ruth's? Or was it simply because Babe was a woman, and her dominating approach to athletics had caused so much controversy?

Through writing and researching Babe's life, we've concluded that the most striking reason was the position taken by the Women's Division of the National Amateur Athletic Federation. The group had been successful in campaigning against competitive sports for girls. Its influence kept sports suppressed for fifty years, and that meant fewer avenues for women athletes.

Two decades after Babe's death, it would not have been unusual to walk into a public-school gymnasium during girls' physical education class and see square dancing instead of basketball. Babe would have rolled her eyes and called the exercise a "sissy" activity.

The real growth of women's sports began after the federal law called Title IX was passed in 1972. The law required publicly funded institutions to offer equal programming for both sexes. It took nearly three more decades (and more than four decades after Babe's death) before a truly successful U.S. women's professional basketball league emerged.

Hired by ESPN to report on the Women's National Basketball Association (WNBA), Sandra Neil Wallace witnessed Babe's drive in many of the players during those early years of women's pro basketball. They performed with a sustained intensity not always seen in the NBA. Many of the U.S. women had played in European professional leagues for low pay, taking other jobs between seasons to help them earn a living, as Babe once had to do. Now they played in a league of their own with a growing fan base to support it.

"I saw in many of those players what I feel is as much a feminine trait as masculine: the desire, like Babe, to support their families," Sandra says. "But I have never known an athlete who was as driven to be a world champion in so many sports for so long as Babe was."

Although Babe is not remembered as well as Babe Ruth is, women's professional sports associations and leagues, from the LPGA to the WNBA, can be traced to Babe's spirit. They inspire young women to make the dream of becoming a professional athlete come true.

Babe's legacy goes way beyond sports. Shortly after her death, the *New York Times* wrote this about her: "This greatest woman athlete of our time has left us a rich heritage. It isn't just in the record books. It is in the inspiring story of a warm human being who had to do it the hard way and who did it magnificently. . . . It is not only the annals of sport that her life has enriched. It is the whole story of human beings who some-how have to keep on trying."

—*RW* and *SNW*

TIMELINE

1911	Born June 26 as Mildred Ella Didriksen in Port Arthur, Texas.
1914–18	*World War I.*
1929	*Great Depression begins.*
1930	Leaves Beaumont High School to join Employers Casualty Company. Wins national titles in javelin and baseball throws.
1930–32	Named to the national basketball all-America team.
1931	Leads Employers Casualty to national basketball title. Sets world record in baseball throw.
1932	Wins national track-and-field championship as one-woman team. Earns two gold medals and one silver in Olympic Games. Named Woman Athlete of the Year by Associated Press. Turns professional.
1935	Wins Texas State Women's Golf Championship.
1938	Meets wrestler George Zaharias and marries him the same year.
1939–45	*World War II.*
1943	Regains amateur status in golf.

1945	*United Nations founded.*
1945–46–47	**Named Woman Athlete of the Year by Associated Press.**
1946–47	**Wins twelve straight golf tournaments.**
1947	**Wins British Women's Amateur title. Turns professional again.**
1949	**Cofounds Ladies' Professional Golf Players Association (later the Ladies Professional Golf Association).**
1950	**Named Woman Athlete of the Year by Associated Press. Voted top woman athlete of the half century.**
1950–53	*Korean War.*
1953	**Diagnosed with cancer.**
1954	**Wins U.S. Women's Open. Named Woman Athlete of the Year by Associated Press.**
1956	**Dies September 27.**
1999	**Named the top woman athlete of the twentieth century by the Associated Press, ESPN, *Sports Illustrated*, and others.**

FREQUENTLY ASKED QUESTIONS

Do any of Babe's track-and-field records still stand?

Yes. Her world record of 296 feet in the baseball throw was never broken. The event was discontinued in 1957.

How much money did Babe make in her lifetime of sports?

More than a million dollars. She was the first woman athlete to reach that mark. She earned it through tournaments, appearance fees, barnstorming, and sponsorships.

Where are Babe's medals and trophies?

In 1976, the Babe Didrikson Zaharias Museum was built in her hometown of Beaumont, Texas. The circular building contains many of Babe's golf trophies and track-and-field medals. Other memorabilia on display at the museum includes photos, sports uniforms, and the scrapbooks maintained by Babe's mother, sister Lillie, and George's friend and assistant, Sid Marks. Admission to the museum is free.

Is there still a Babe Didrikson Zaharias Golf Tournament?

The tournament ran on the LPGA circuit for many years. Today, a local tournament in Beaumont is played in Babe's honor to raise money for the Babe Didrikson Zaharias Foundation. The general public is invited to play.

Where are Babe's letters to Tiny Scurlock kept?

Tiny kept all the letters he and Babe had written to each other since her high school days. He also filled boxes with notes and clippings about his favorite athlete. Tiny had hoped to write a book about Babe someday but never did. Thanks to his wife and Babe's former English teacher, Ruth Scurlock, all letters, photos, and mementos were donated to Lamar University in Beaumont.

Along with Babe's autobiography, they offer insight into Babe's feelings about her life and accomplishments.

Babe had a close relationship with Betty Dodd. Were they gay?

Babe challenged society's idea of femininity because she performed in sports commonly associated with men. But although Babe admitted to friends and family that her marriage to George had soured, there was no such talk about being a lesbian. A biographer has speculated that Babe was in a lesbian relationship with golfer Betty Dodd. If she was, Betty and Babe kept the relationship private. No colleagues or family members have acknowledged that the two were lovers. Babe and George remained married, and he was with her until she died.

What became of George Zaharias after Babe died?

George sold Rainbow Manor but remained in Tampa, Florida. Just before Babe's death, George made plans to sponsor a traveling trophy for the Associated Press Woman Athlete of the Year, which Babe had won six times. It became known as the Babe Didrikson Zaharias Trophy. George also had a replica made of Babe's silver trophy from the 1947 British Women's Amateur and donated it to a school tournament in Gullane, Scotland. Children still compete for the trophy each summer. George's health declined and he lost most of his eyesight. He married the nurse who took care of him. He died in 1984.

What became of Babe's sister Lillie?

Lillie remained in Beaumont, Texas, in a house not far from Doucette Avenue. She married O. B. Grimes and had three children. Lillie remained devoted to Babe, even after her sister's death, and visited the gravesite weekly. When Lillie died in 1983, she was buried near Babe.

Who looked after Babe's poodle, Bebe, after Babe died?

Lillie took in the poodle. She enjoyed its company for many years. Ruth Scurlock, Babe's longtime friend, kept in touch with Lillie after

Babe's death. Ruth said that when the poodle died, Lillie felt a deep loss. She'd seen the poodle as another connection to her sister.

Is the Didriksen house still standing in Beaumont?

The house still stands on Doucette Avenue, but it was not occupied in 2013 and had a chain-link fence around the property. You can still see the front porch where Babe played the harmonica and the side porch she scrubbed on Saturdays. The hedges Babe hurdled on Doucette are gone. The Magnolia Refinery is still there, though. Now owned by ExxonMobil, it is less than five blocks from the former Didriksen home.

Where is Babe buried?

Babe is buried at Forest Lawn Memorial Park, near the Beaumont Country Club, where she first learned how to play golf in high school, dodging snakes on the sandy greens. A marble podium stands by Babe's grave, with an open marble book and this inscription made famous by sportswriter Grantland Rice: "It's not whether you win or lose, but how you played the game." Nothing could be further from the truth when it came to Babe. She played to win. The nearby steel marker put up by the Texas Historical Commission is inaccurate, too. It states that Babe was named after Babe Ruth and that her birth year was 1914. Both the story and the date were fabricated by Babe. The year etched on her gravestone, however, is accurate. "I figured that's goin' to be there till the hereafter," said Lillie, who made sure that date was correct. "I wasn't goin' to have it wrong."

How is Babe remembered today?

In addition to the Babe Didrikson Zaharias Museum and golf trophies named in her honor, there are other tributes to Babe. In Beaumont, a park and stadium are named for her. There is also a street called Babe Didrikson Zaharias Drive in Beaumont. In 1975, a movie capturing Babe's life, called *Babe*, was made by MGM.

SOURCE NOTES*

The source of each quotation in this book is found below. The citation indicates the first words of the quotation and its document source. Most sources are listed in the bibliography. For those not listed, complete citations are provided below.

The following abbreviations are used:

INCREDIBLE (*The Incredible Babe: Her Ultimate Story* by Thad S. Johnson with Louis Didrikson)

LAMAR (Lamar University Special Collections and Archives: Babe Didrikson Zaharias Collection)

LIFE (*This Life I've Led* by Babe Didrikson Zaharias with Harry Paxton)

NYT (*New York Times*)

WG (*"Whatta-Gal": The Babe Didrikson Story* by William Oscar Johnson and Nancy P. Williamson)

The Opening Pitch (Authors' Note) (page 8)
"Just where fact ends . . .": William Scurlock notes, LAMAR, 11.1.2.14.

Round 1 (page 14)
"All my life . . .": LIFE, p. 30.
"If she beat me . . .": WG, p. 54.
"the most disastrous . . .": *Beaumont Journal*, June 26, 1911.
"nothin' but oil, oil, oil": WG, p. 38.
"How is it . . .": INCREDIBLE, p. 81.
"We was so scared . . .": WG, p. 39.
"Some of us opened . . .": INCREDIBLE, p. 118.
"Poppa let Momma handle . . .": LIFE, p. 9.
"callin' and *callin'* . . .": WG, p. 43.
"hugged Babe up": same as above, p.11.
"What a bang . . .": LIFE, p. 8.
"full of devilment": WG, pp. 43–44.
"a little Tartar . . ." and "always honest . . .": interview with Emma Andress, LAMAR, 11.1.1.20.
"too good to compete . . ." and "too far ahead . . .": interview with Piland, LAMAR, 11.1.12.2.
"in right field . . ." and "Babe was different . . .": WG, p. 54.
"Babe never saw . . .": INCREDIBLE, p. 64.
"was the ringleader . . .": same as above, p. 63.

"keep your bowels clear": WG, p. 37.

"get in there and work . . .": LIFE, p. 7.

"skate[d] around on the soap suds and "[Momma would] take . . .": same as above, p. 21.

"A couple of minutes . . .": same as above, p. 25.

"had done so much . . .": same as above, p. 7.

Racism in Beaumont

"morality, Americanism, . . .": Rienstra and Linsley, p. 64.

Round 2 (page 36)

"Before I was even . . .": LIFE, p. 27.

"Inherent evils . . .": WG, p. 31.

"She was the best . . .": same as above, p. 43.

"and then I'd work . . .": LIFE, p. 27.

"came out on . . .": same as above, p. 16.

"suspended by her teeth . . ." and "human aerial top": *Ringling Brothers Route Books 1898*, circushistory.org.

"slide for life": Ringling Museum, May 5, 1923, p. 76.

"on our heads . . .": LIFE, p. 13.

"afraid of something . . ." and "didn't learn a thing": WG, p. 45.

"the home room . . .": interview with E. W. Jackson, LAMAR, 11.1.1.19.

"tell those women . . .": LIFE, p. 33.

"was blessed . . .": WG, p. 58.

"and I went into my fighting stance . . .": INCREDIBLE, p. 174.

"With one dribble . . .": interview with Lytle, LAMAR, p. 8.

"overwhelming majority . . .": WG, p. 55.

"down to where . . .": LIFE, p. 29.

"just goes in for games . . .": WG, p. 51.

"growing aversity . . .": 1929 *Pine Burr* yearbook, LAMAR.

"extremely strenuous physical . . .": WG, p. 31.

"let her try . . ." and "flat against letting . . .": same as above, p. 54.

"Sports was a way . . .": same as above, p. 55.

Round 3 (page 58)

"She was out . . .": WG, p. 75.

"It came time to announce . . .": LIFE, p. 48.

"just for carrying . . .": same as above, p. 4.

"never . . . seen a man or woman . . .": WG, p. 78.

"prolonged and intense strain": same as above, p. 33.

"suitable costumes": Women's Division of the National Amateur Athletic Federation statement of principles.

"never seen so many . . ." and "got a little pepped up" and "Well, that's what . . .": LIFE, p. 36.

"*Dear Tiny: Played my first* . . .": Babe, letter to Tiny Scurlock, February 19, 1930, LAMAR, 11.1.14.1.

"still knocking them cold" and "We have two . . .": Babe, letter to Tiny Scurlock, LAMAR, March 6, 1930, 11.1.14.3.

"I have a whole lots . . .": Babe, letter to Tiny Scurlock, March 19, 1930, LAMAR, 11.1.14.4.

"I have had two more . . .": Babe, letter to Tiny Scurlock, March 6, 1930, LAMAR, 11.1.14.3.

"if I can help it": Babe, letter to Tiny Scurlock, February 21, 1930, LAMAR, 11.1.14.2.

"I wasn't spending . . .": LIFE, p. 39.

"a little bitty sink": WG, p. 67.

"You could choose . . ." and "I really felt bad . . .": LIFE, p. 38.

"withdrew to play . . .": INCREDIBLE, p. 164.

"this stick lying . . ." and "got pretty good distance . . .": LIFE, p. 40.

"We all got together . . ." and "jog[ging] my legs . . .": same as above, p. 41.

"Her only fault . . .": WG, p. 78.

"It was that last . . .": LIFE, p. 42.

"Your feet had to . . .": same as above, p. 57.

"gouged around . . .": Babe, letter to Tiny Scurlock, June 23, 1930, LAMAR.

"*Oh! yeah! right after* . . .": same as above.

"Her favorite color . . .": LAMAR, 11.1.1.4.

"She always had . . .": LAMAR, 11.1.1.19.

"Babe broke the world record . . .": *Los Angeles Mirror*, September 28, 1956.

"took first place away . . .": LIFE, p. 44.

"exploited [Babe] for their own . . .": interview with Lytle, LAMAR, p. 3.

"Babe's family . . .": WG, p. 77.

"are plenty nice . . ." and "*Write me a letter* . . .": Babe, letter to Tiny Scurlock, April 25, 1931, LAMAR, 11.1.14.10.

"I admit I admired . . .": WG, p. 75.

"*Dearest Tiny—Heck I'm tired* . . .": Babe, letter to Tiny Scurlock, October 5, 1931, LAMAR, 11.1.14.12.

"I won't try to play . . .": Babe, letter to Tiny Scurlock, December 28, 1931, LAMAR, 11.1.14.14.

"one-girl track team": Van Natta.

"would just bounce . . .": LIFE, p. 47.

"You never heard . . .": same as above, pp. 48–49.

"We suddenly heard . . .": WG, p. 81.

"while last year . . .": *Beaumont Journal*, July 1932.

"It was one of those . . .": LIFE, p. 48.

"The judges huddled . . .": WG, p. 82.

"under prolonged and intense . . .": same as above, p. 33.

"The most amazing series . . ." and "Such assistance as . . .": same as above, p. 83.

A Roadblock for Women

"A team for everyone . . .": WG, p. 29.

Women in the Olympics

"As to the admission . . .": WG, p. 33.

Round 4 (page 94)

"I came out here . . .": Smith, p. 11.

"If there is anything . . .": Pieroth, p. 5.

"started beating her chest . . .": WG, p. 84.

"Most of the girls . . .": LIFE, p. 52.

"impossible to get . . .": WG, p. 85.

"They especially liked . . .": same as above, p. 84.

"If Babe had won . . .": same as above, p. 85.

"eleven wretched women": *Running Times*, May 14, 2012.

"for the opportunity . . .": WG, p. 33.

"While their records . . .": Pieroth, p. 85.

"a woman's place . . .": same as above, p. 101.

"prevented from cluttering . . .": same as above.

"male athletes . . .": Pieroth, p. 97.

"provide a refreshing . . .": same as above.

"I came out here . . .": Smith, p. 11.

"What I want to do . . .": WG, p. 99.

"To set it aside . . .": Pieroth, p. 97.

"You see people . . .": same as above, p. 91.

"Here I was . . .": same as above, p. 90.

"The greatest girl athlete . . .": "Women and Sports," *Literary Digest*, August 27, 1932.

"Athletics are all I care for . . .": Associated Press, July 1932, LAMAR, 11.1.4.6.

"So you're the big shot . . .": *Beaumont Enterprise*, August 17, 1932.

"Folks say that . . .": WG, p. 100.

Babe's Best Foes

"I really was a daredevil . . .": Hodak, interview with Hall Adams, p. 2.

"I think the greatest . . .": same as above.

Round 5 (page 110)

"Didrikson leaps . . .": *Los Angeles Mirror*, September 28, 1956.

"Win the next . . .": Pieroth, p. 109.

"Just for once . . .": *Los Angeles Times*; WG, p. 103.

"I couldn't enjoy . . .": LIFE, p. 53.

"shadows were coming up . . ." and "My hand slipped . . .": same as above, p. 54–55.

"Nobody knew it . . .": same as above, p. 55.

"A woman athlete . . .": Daley, July 31, 1932.

"refusing to take . . .": LIFE, p. 53.

"The irrepressible . . .": Daley, August 4, 1932.

"held back . . .": LIFE, p. 55.

"Hall was a yard . . .": *Los Angeles Mirror*, September 28, 1956.

"'Well, I won'": WG, p. 105.

"Yep, I'm going to win . . .": Associated Press; WG, p. 100.

"Both of us . . .": LIFE, p. 56.

"spring in her legs": Pieroth, p. 112.

"We couldn't beat her . . .": WG, p. 107.

"The pit was sand . . .": Hodak, interview with Shiley Newhouse, p. 24.

"I just soared . . .": LIFE, p. 56.

"all twisted": WG, p. 106.

"The collection is . . .": "Women and Sports," *Literary Digest*, August 27, 1932.

"All of her jumps . . .": WG, p. 107.

"They had a party . . .": Hodak, interview with Shiley Newhouse, p. 23.

"Everyone agreed . . .": "Babe, Heralded Like Lindbergh . . .", 1932, LAMAR, 11.1.4.14.

"No nicer girl . . .": LAMAR, scrapbook files.

"I was riding . . .": LIFE, p. 63.

"Oh, I got *up* there . . .": WG, pp. 108–109.

"She is beyond . . .": *Beaumont Journal*, August 14, 1932, LAMAR, 11.1.1.8.

The Hooverville Olympics

"completely equipped . . ." NYT, July 30, 1932.

"blossomed out" and "stores and hotels . . .": Hall.

Round 6 (page 136)

"People kept telling me . . .": LIFE, p. 68.

"Miss Didrikson is probably . . .": Daley, January 5, 1933.

"the Texas tornado's": "Women and Sports," *Literary Digest*, August 27, 1932.

"She steps up . . ." and "for a man . . .": LAMAR, 11.1.1.8.

"Gallico and I paid off . . .": same as above.

"and, what's more . . .": WG, p. 6.

"would have been fair . . ." and "sorry about . . .": LIFE, p. 69.

"a terrifying business" and "I'm afraid . . .": NYT, December 24, 1932.

"the ancient Greeks . . .": NYT, December 25, 1932.

"My Lord, I can't . . .": LIFE, p. 70.

"They staged it . . .": same as above, p. 71.

"Friday afternoon . . .": *Chicago Tribune*; Cayleff, p. 103.

"It was still in . . .": LIFE, p. 72–73.

"I never got pushed . . ." and "all fired up . . .": same as above, p. 76.

"I tried to keep . . ." and "Momma and Poppa were . . ." and "I was going to do . . .": same as above, p. 77.

"She hit ball after . . .": Lader.

"pitches with a . . .": McGowen.

"Sometimes, . . . I wasn't . . .": LIFE, photo caption between pp. 34–35.

"was terribly hard . . .": WG, p. 128–129.

"My name had meant . . .": LIFE, p. 85.

The Writer behind the "Muscle Moll"

"She was a pathetic . . .": Cayleff, p.138.

"because she would not . . .": Gallico, *Vanity Fair*; Van Natta, p. 140.

"Muscle Moll": Cayleff, p. 86.

"I loved to play . . .": WG, p. 132.

"I'm afraid that we often . . .": Gallico, LAMAR, 11.1.13.16.

Round 7 (page 160)

"Most things come natural . . .": North American Newspaper Alliance, 1933; Cayleff, p. 118.

"She had a slight . . .": interview with Lytle, LAMAR, p. 16.

"She was so poor . . .": Cayleff, p. 129.

"It did me good . . .": LIFE, p. 87.

"No prize I've won . . .": same as above, p. 88.

"I settled into . . .": same as above, p. 87.

"I'd go to bed . . .": same as above, p. 89.

"We really don't need . . .": Van Natta, p. 166.

"it wasn't ladylike . . ." and "There's where . . .": Wakeman, p. 59.

"Everybody was saying . . .": LIFE, p. 94.

"I studied that shot . . .": same as above, p. 95.

"'Best at Everything' . . .": *Newsweek*; Cayleff, p. 125.

"a swell girl": LIFE, photo caption between pp. 34–35.

"It seemed they'd . . .": same as above, p. 96.

"activities as a professional . . .": Cayleff, p. 125.

"I'd never been a . . .": LIFE, p. 91.

"The galleries were . . .": Cayleff, p. 118.

"Don't you men . . .": Wakeman, p. 64.

"I'll break my neck . . .": LIFE, p. 100.

"I'd kid him . . .": same as above, p. 99.

"Some writers have said . . .": and "But I was . . .": same as above, pp. 103–104.

"concentrate on my golf . . .": same as above, p. 102.

"One day when he broke . . .": same as above, p. 105.

Round 8 (page 178)

"She wasn't just . . .": Smith, p. 84.

"He was a great actor . . .": WG, p. 160.

"He put his arm . . ." LIFE, p. 105.

"When we shook hands . . .": Cayleff, p. 135.

"Those people didn't . . .": LIFE, p. 106.

"I already had . . .": same as above, p. 107.

"The fans hate me . . .": Cayleff, p. 136.

"Listen, George Zaharias . . .": WG, p. 160.

"But that particular . . .": Cayleff, p. 138.

"We're going to get . . .": LIFE, p. 111.

"When I first put . . .": Stronger, January 17, 1973, LAMAR 11.2.4.2.

"Here I'd been practicing . . .": LIFE, p. 119.

"settled down to . . .": Cayleff, p. 144.

"I had to stay . . ." and "was a top bean . . .": LIFE, p. 119.

"There was hardly . . .": Cayleff, p. 145.

"In the space . . ." and "'The deuce with it'": Daley, June 8, 1947.

"Naturally it . . .": LIFE, p. 125.

"I wasn't going . . .": same as above, p. 127.

"There's only one . . .": Cayleff, p. 147.

"Babe, if I cried, . . .": LIFE, p. 138.

"I didn't feel like . . ." and "Your Momma wants . . ." and "But with the wartime . . .": same as above, p. 136.

"Babe just sat there . . .": Cayleff, pp. 150–151.

"felt I was playing . . .": same as above, p. 151.

"I never could cry . . .": LIFE, p. 138.

"build that streak . . .": Cayleff, p. 167.

"I'm tired of traveling . . ." and "No, honey . . .": LIFE, p. 144.

"I won't go . . ." and "Sure, honey . . ." and "I know you . . .": same as above, p. 147.

Going for Broke

"She talked to me . . .": Newport, WSJ.com.

Round 9 (page 200)

"Before Babe it was . . .": Cayleff, p. 159.

"She was very . . .": Wallace and Wallace, interview with Andrew.

"I'd seen many golfers . . .": Wallace and Wallace, interview with Craigs.

"went to an American boat . . .": LIFE, p. 153.

"When I walked back . . .": same as above, p. 154.

"When I practiced . . .": same as above, p. 155.

"Well, I've got to . . ." and "thumb stayed sore . . .": same as above, p. 157.

"well played" and "nice shot": same as above, p. 162.

"I began kidding them . . .": same as above, p. 162.

"like a small cannon . . .": same as above, p. 163.

"Probably more so . . .": Wallace and Wallace, interview with Craigs.

"Scottish people are . . .": same as above.

"She just brought . . .": same as above.

"[Babe] was tremendous . . .": Wallace and Wallace, interview with Andrew.

"Babe, go git . . .": LIFE, p. 171.

"But I didn't do it . . .": same as above, p. 172.

"a little Highland song . . .": same as above, p. 175.

"It got to the point . . .": same as above, p. 180.

"I spent a short . . .": Cayleff, p. 177.

"She had a flair . . .": same as above, p. 180.

"That was the one . . .": LIFE, p. 185.

"Women's golf belongs . . .": Cayleff, p. 188.

"*I'm* the star . . .": WG, p. 190.

"She made it . . .": Cayleff, p. 194.

"was never charged . . .": same as above, p. 183.

"Babe remained . . .": same as above, p. 190.

"Oh, how she . . ." and "[I] couldn't have hit . . .": same as above, p. 163.

"Would she try . . .": Van Natta, p. 267.

"spent considerable time . . .": NYT, September 28, 1956.

"After a while . . .": Cayleff, p. 199.

"He wanted to . . .": same as above, p. 198.

"We always had . . .": same as above, p. 203.

"We started getting . . .": INCREDIBLE, p. 389.

"Doctor Tatum told me . . .": LIFE, p. 191.

"Then I knocked . . ." and "As soon as I . . .": same as above, p. 196.

"Then he probed . . .": same as above, p. 197.

"Something Altogether Different"

Information and quotations from Wallace interviews with Rena (Walker) Craigs and Gratian (Salvesen) Andrew, March 2013.

Best of the Century

"During all those years . . .": LIFE, p. 139.

The Final Round (page 226)

"I don't know yet . . .": Associated Press; Van Natta, p. 297.

"I was determined . . .": LIFE, p. 5.

"like a thunderbolt" and "I thought I was . . .": same as above, p. 201.

"I won't be needing . . .": same as above, p. 202.

"fabulous career . . .": WG, p. 204.

"I made up my mind . . ." and "I believe the cancer . . .": LIFE, p. 5.

"changed permanently . . .": same as above, p. 208.

"I don't care what . . .": same as above, p. 205.

"First they were . . .": same as above, p. 206.

"I'm tired . . .": "Babe Zaharias Goes Under Knife," 1953, LAMAR, 11.1.6.13.

"colostomy, honey?" and "Yes. It's all right": LIFE, p. 211.

"I didn't know exactly . . .": same as above, p. 212.

"I have never been . . .": same as above, pp. 209–210.

"did have faith . . .": interview with Scurlock, LAMAR, p. 16.

"I started raising . . .": LIFE, p. 213.

"A colostomy is . . .": same as above, p. 217.

"Let's go play . . ." and "I don't want . . ." and "Guess I gotta . . .":
    WG, p. 208.

"You go out . . .": Van Natta, p. 305.

"It seemed like I . . .": LIFE, p. 6.

"Babe, quit . . ." and "I'm not a quitter": WG, p. 209.

"To me, shooting . . .": LIFE, p. 217.

"with all I've got.": Van Natta, p. 306.

"People were beginning . . .": LIFE, p. 219.

"Those letters . . .": same as above, p. 218.

"I guess I'll have to . . .": NYT, February 22, 1954.

"All boys are . . .": Van Natta, p. 309.

"the most incredible . . .": Murray.

"I'm happy because . . .": Van Natta, p. 312.

"That was her greatest . . .": interview with Scurlock, LAMAR, p. 14.

"You did it yourself . . .": Cayleff, p. 227.

"when all of us . . .": LIFE, p. 229.

"You've proved . . .": Van Natta, p. 317.

"At times . . .": LIFE, p. 228.

"There are several . . .": same as above.

"With the love . . .": LIFE, p. 232.

"I just wanted . . .": Van Natta, p. 323.

"I was dying to win . . .": WG, p. 216.

"held my hand . . .": same as above, p. 217.

"I know she'll . . .": *Beaumont Journal*, September 27, 1956, LAMAR,
    11.1.9.3.

"She didn't know . . .": NYT, September 28, 1956.

"She was always . . .": Associated Press, September 29, 1956.

Post-Match (Authors' Note) (page 246)

"This greatest woman athlete . . .": NYT, September 28, 1956.

Frequently Asked Questions (page 254)

"I figured that's goin' to be there . . .": WG, p. 35.

BIBLIOGRAPHY

Associated Press. "Babe Didrikson of Dallas, Olympic Prospect, Holds Eight Track Records." July 1932.

Barney, Robert K. "Resistance, Persistence, Providence: The 1932 Los Angeles Olympic Games in Perspective." *Research Quarterly for Exercise and Sport* 67, no. 2, June 1996.

Beaumont Enterprise. "Babe Didrikson Is Honor Guest at Luncheon." August 17, 1932.

___. "Great Storm Lashes Gulf Coast." August 17, 1915.

___. "Port Arthur in Great Danger." August 18, 1915.

Beaumont Journal. "'Broadway Welcome' Planned by City of Dallas to Honor Babe's Return." August 6, 1932.

___. "Cancer Claims Life of Babe Zaharias." September 27, 1956.

___. "Dallas Proud of Mildred." July 1932.

___. "Grant Says Babe Is Marvel." August 14, 1932.

Bredeson, Carmen. *The Spindletop Gusher: The Story of the Texas Oil Boom.* Houston: Bright Sky Press, 2010.

Burton, Rick. "Searching for Sports' First Female Pitchman." *New York Times*, January 1, 2011.

Cayleff, Susan E. *Babe: The Life and Legend of Babe Didrikson Zaharias.* Urbana: University of Illinois Press, 1995.

Cunningham, Bill. "The Colonel's Ladies." *Collier's*, May 23, 1936.

Daley, Arthur J. "Babe Didrikson, Visiting Here, Hopes to Box Babe Ruth in Gym." *New York Times*, January 5, 1933.

___. "Beccali of Italy Wins 1,500 Meters at Olympic Games." *New York Times*, August 5, 1932.

___. "Four U.S. Athletes Win Olympic Titles as 85,000 Look On." *New York Times*, August 4, 1932.

___. "A Look on the Distaff Side." *New York Times*, June 8, 1947.

___. "A Remarkable Woman." *New York Times*, September 30, 1956.

___. "Zabala, Argentina, Wins the Marathon; Sets Olympic Mark." *New York Times*, August 8, 1932.

Danzig, Allison. "Curtis Proclaims the Olympics Open as 100,000 Look On." *New York Times*, July 31, 1932.

___. "Indian Team Shines at Field Hockey." *New York Times*, August 5, 1932.

___. "Thousands Crowding into Los Angeles for Opening of Olympic Games Tomorrow." *New York Times*, July 29, 1932.

Gallico, Paul. *The Golden People.* Garden City, NY: Doubleday, 1965.

___. "The Texas Babe." *Vanity Fair*, October 1932.

___. "This Man's World." *Esquire*, March 1955.

Guttmann, Allen. *Women's Sports: A History*. New York: Columbia University Press, 1991.

Hall, Chapin. "Los Angeles Rises Above Depression." *New York Times*, August 7, 1932.

Hodak, George A. Interview with Evelyne Hall Adams, October 1987. Amateur Athletic Foundation of Los Angeles.

___. Interview with Jean Shiley Newhouse. Lamar University archives, undated.

Ikard, Robert W. *Just for Fun: The Story of AAU Women's Basketball*. Fayetteville: University of Arkansas Press, 2005.

Johnson, Thad S. *The Incredible Babe: Her Ultimate Story*. With Louis Didrikson. Lake Charles, LA: published by author, 1996.

Johnson, William Oscar, and Nancy P. Williamson. *"Whatta-Gal": The Babe Didrikson Story*. Boston: Little, Brown, 1975.

Lader, Lawrence. "The Unbeatable Babe." *Coronet*, January 1948.

Lamar University Special Collections and Archives. Interview with Bea Lytle, undated.

___. Interview with Effie Piland, undated.

___. Interview with Emma Andress, undated.

___. Interview with Mrs. A. J. Harmon, undated.

___. Interview with Ruth Scurlock, undated.

Los Angeles Mirror. "Babe Didrikson." September 28, 1956.

McGowen, Roscoe. "Dodgers Conquer Athletics by 4–2." *New York Times*, March 21, 1934.

Murray, Jim. "The Other Babe." *Los Angeles Times*.

Newport, John Paul. "Palmer's Go-for-It Greatness." *Wall Street Journal*, September 11, 2009.

New York Times. "Babe Didrikson Barred by A.A.U." December 6, 1932.

___. "Babe Zaharias Dies; Athlete Had Cancer." September 28, 1956.

___. "Camps Now Charred Ruins." July 30, 1932.

___. "Curtis Formally Opens Olympic Games." July 31, 1932.

___. "Five First Places to Miss Didrikson." July 17, 1932.

___. "Greeks Were Right, Brundage Believes." December 25, 1932.

___. "Hoover Observes Olympic Custom." July 30, 1932.

___. "Mid-Century Poll to Mrs. Zaharias." February 16, 1950.

___. "Miss Didrikson Adheres to Plans." December 24, 1932.

___. "Miss Didrikson, Olympic Athlete, Is Named Outstanding Woman Performer of the Year." December 20, 1932.

___. "Miss Didrikson, the One-Girl Track Team, Heads U.S. Squad of 16 Named for Olympics." July 18, 1932.

___. "Miss Didrikson to Play in U.S. Title Golf; Dallas Welcomes Olympic Star with Parade." August 12, 1932.

___. "1932 Olympic Receipts Listed as $1,483,535." July 19, 1933.

___. "Olympic Schedule for 1932 Announced." June 22, 1931.

___. "Starting Blocks Banned in Games." July 28, 1932.

___. "Suggest Olympics Should Be Put Off." September 24, 1931.

___. "Veterans Barred from White House." July 21, 1932.

Pieroth, Doris H. *Their Day in the Sun: Women of the 1932 Olympics*. Seattle: University of Washington Press, 1996.

Rice, Grantland. *The Tumult and the Shouting: My Life in Sport*. New York: Barnes, 1954.

Rienstra, Ellen Walker, and Judith Walker Linsley. *Historic Beaumont: An Illustrated History*. San Antonio: Historical Publishing Network, 2003.

Robinson, Roger. "'Eleven Wretched Women': What Really Happened in the First Olympic Women's 800m." *Running Times*, May 14, 2012.

Scurlock, Bill. "Babe Looking for Grand Slam." *Beaumont Journal*, July 8, 1932.

___. "Parents May Go to Dallas to Greet Babe." *Beaumont Journal*, August 11, 1932.

Smith, Lissa, ed. *Nike Is a Goddess: The History of Women in Sports*. New York: Atlantic Monthly Press, 1998.

Stronger, Karol. "George Goes On without Babe." Associated Press, January 17, 1973.

Van Natta, Don, Jr. *Wonder Girl: The Magnificent Sporting Life of Babe Didrikson Zaharias*. New York: Little, Brown, 2011.

Wakeman, Nancy. *Babe Didrikson Zaharias: Driven to Win*. Minneapolis: Lerner Publications, 2000.

Wallace, Rich, and Sandra Neil Wallace. Interview with Gratian (Salvesen) Andrew, March 2013.

___. Interview with Rena (Walker) Craigs, March 2013.

Zaharias, Babe Didrikson. *This Life I've Led: An Autobiography*. With Harry Paxton. New York: Barnes, 1955.

FOR MORE INFORMATION *

Babe Didrikson Zaharias Museum, Beaumont, Texas. babedidriksonzaharias.org
Ladies Professional Golf Association. lpga.com
United States Golf Association. usga.org
U.S. Olympic Committee. teamusa.org
Women's National Basketball Association. wnba.com
Women's Sports Foundation. womenssportsfoundation.org

*All websites active at time of publication

INDEX

Page numbers in **boldface** refer to photographs and/or captions.

PICTURE CREDITS

©**Associated Press**: 8, 80. 199.

Babe Didrikson Zaharias Museum, Beaumont, Texas: 17, 30, 60, 63, 78–79, 116, 162, 164, 172–173, 178, 187, 197, 222 (bottom), 249.

©**Bettmann/CORBIS**: front jacket, 2–3, 110, 128–129, 154, 160, 169, 176–177, 184–185.

Bibliothèque nationale de France: 93.

familyphotos.com: 21 (top left).

The Granger Collection, New York: ullstein bild: 77, 248; 122–123.

Gullane Ladies Golf Club, East Lothian, Scotland: 213.

Herbert Hoover Presidential Library-Museum: 65, 67.

John and Mable Ringling Museum of Art Tibbals Digital Collection: 41, 42.

Library of Congress, Prints and Photographs Division: LC-USZ62-124536: 5; LC-USZ62-4723: 24 (bottom); LC-DIG-ggbain-17840: 91; LC-USZ62-101582: 96; LC-USZ62-113281: 112; LC-USZ62-52818: 114–115; LC-DIG-hec-36872: 119; LC-USZ62-117470: 142; LC-USZ62-121615: 200; LC-USZ62-77828: 226.

Mary and John Gray Library, Archives and Special Collections, Lamar University, Beaumont, Texas: document 11.2.5.17: 1, 130; 11.2.6.22: 13;. 11.2.22.1: 14, 23; 11.2.5.3: 19; 11.2.22.1: 23; 11.2.5.6: 36, 47; 11.2.5.4: 39; 11.2.5.52: 52; 11.2.5.11: 54; 11.2.5.18: 58, 88–89; 11.2.5.12: 62; 11.1.14.7: 75; 11.1.4.1: 94; 11.2.5.20: 101; 11.2.6.18: 105; 11.2.5.9: 107; 11.2.5.14: 108–109; 11.2.5.24: 134–135; 11.2.5.38: 136, 150–151; 11.1.16.5: 138, 147; 11.2.5.51: 141; 11.2.5.35: 146; 11.2.6.17: 155; 11.2.5.58: 157; 11.2.6.1: 158; 11.2.5.50: 180, 190; 11.2.6.16: 182; 11.2.6.20: 194; 11.1.16.5: 202, 206–207; 11.2.7.9: 203; 11.2.7.25: 216; 11.2.6.25: 222 (top); 11.2.7.16: 224; 11.2.7.27: 228, 238; 11.2.9.7: 230; 11.2.8.13: 233; 11.2.8.28: 235; 11.2.8.37: 246.

Museum of the Gulf Coast: 21 (bottom right).

Texas Energy Museum, Beaumont, Texas: 16, 26–27.

Tyrrell Historical Library, Beaumont, Texas: 24 (top), 28, 34–35, 38, 45, 48–49.

University of Texas at Arlington Library, Special Collections: 166.

TEXT CREDITS

From **The New York Times**, August 4, 1932 (124); January 5, 1933 (138); June 8, 1947 (189); September 28, 1956 (245, 251) © The New York Times. All rights reserved. Used by permission and protected by the Copyright Laws of the United States. The printing, copying, redistribution, or retransmission of this Content without express written permission is prohibited.